CONTENTS

Looking for a use for a Bachmann Class 57, dressed as a 'Delner' coupling-fitted Virgin Trains locomotive? Timber trains from Crianlarich to Chirk were hauled by Class 57s for a time in 2007 and 2008. Virgin Trains Class 57, 57 311 *Parker* trundles south through Carlisle on February 15, 2008. The wagons are cut-down ferry vans, coded KFA, which could be modelled using the Heljan model.

Modern wagons in 4mm scale.
Making the best of ready-to-run models.

As locomotive-hauled trains have declined in number over the last few years, many D&E modellers interested in the modern railway scene have turned their attention to freight operations as a way to provide work for their collections of locomotives. In recent years, there has been a significant increase in the volume of freight hauled on the national rail network, resulting in the introduction of new high-capacity wagons, growth in colourful intermodal operation and a new lease of life for

many older wagons which may otherwise have declined into rust and decay in the engineers' fleet. Fortunately, this growth has been matched by new products from the mainstream manufacturers. Also, recognising wagons seen from the lineside and being able to identify them as modelling projects is a very enjoyable part of the hobby.

With the growth in quality off-the-shelf models at often surprisingly good prices, the modeller can make a start on building a convincing fleet of wagons

straight from the model shop and this task is easier than ever before. However, the standard varies from manufacturer to manufacturer amongst new releases and even within a given range. Some modellers point to the difference in standard between the Bachmann HTA and HHA high capacity coal hoppers and its TTA tank wagon as an example of differing standards. To be fair, the difference is also reflected in the price, and leaves much opportunity for refinement and customisation – each model is seen as a modelling opportunity and modelling is what it is all about after all!

Older models such as the Hornby PCA depressed centre tank wagon, together with its PGA aggregate hopper, all provide an opportunity for detailing and refinement, whilst re-issued models from former ranges such as Lima bring a welcome return of old favourites, all of which have a place.

A frequently asked question from newcomers to the hobby is how to convincingly model a fleet of wagons representing modern operations from the BR sectorisation era to the present day? It's a big question, and I have presented this book in a style to help both the newcomer and experienced modeller make the best of ready-to-run wagons. Whilst it is not possible to provide detail on every variation (there are many books written on the development and use of full-size rail wagons), it has been written to provide

Didcot is the location of this picture of 60 030, which was working with HGA hopper wagons commonly used on ballast duties or aggregate traffic. HGA wagons are former 'Gunnells' converted from the PGA wagon fleet. They can be modelled using the former Lima PGA hopper as a starting point.

inspiration, outline prototype information and ideas on how to make the best use of those ready-to-run models currently available from the mainstream manufacturers. Most importantly, I hope it adds to the enjoyment of creating something that is uniquely yours and you gain satisfaction from placing the detailed and customised wagons on your layout to provide a freight service to your on line customers!

Not all MGR coal trains operate to power stations. This short set of hopper wagons was bound for the cement works at Westbury when photographed on May 7, 2004, with 60 031 in charge. The train is a mix of open hoppers and those modified with canopies, albeit very bashed-in. This train can easily be modelled using Hornby products.

Millbrook is the location of this photograph of a short train of TTA tank wagons which were being transferred between Eastleigh and the Esso refinery at Fawley behind 66 073 on December 2, 2003. Bachmann produces both the locomotive and wagons in 4mm scale. The Bachmann tank wagon model can be detailed to a high standard with replacement buffers, suspension details and etched-brass walkways and ladders.

There has always been a 'cottage industry' based around supplying detailing and conversion parts for locomotives. This has, to some extent, been mirrored with rolling stock too including wagons, the small manufacturers producing wagon kits and making components taken from them available for sale as separate items, which has done much to help the modern D&E modeller to achieve some great results with ready-to-run wagons.

There is nothing to stop you from using the amazing variety of detailing components and finishing products to customise, detail and adapt the various kits and ready-to-run models that are currently available. Genesis Kits, Inter-City Models, 51L Models and S Kits all offer a variety of components to enhance modern wagons and these components are as diverse as buffers, air brake equipment, axle guards, suspension springs, coupling hooks, air hoses, brake blocks and shoes, bolsters, bogie kits - there is a great deal of trade support available.

Finishing products are available from Fox Transfers, Modelmaster Professional, Phoenix Precision Paints and Railmatch, all of which can be used to repaint existing models and apply new transfers to renumber them. Do not forget to add weathering powders, weathering paint colours and varnish to your shopping list. Part of customising your fleet will be to weather the models convincingly using reference photographs to see how they accumulate grime or slowly rust away!

It is worth taking time to locate the source of good quality detailing and conversion parts and they may be as simple as replacement buffers, air tanks, air cylinders, air brake distribution valves and various parts for the wagon suspension. The parts I most commonly use on my wagon projects which are purchased from small suppliers include:

- Cast metal wagon bogies
- Replacement buffers in brass and white metal
- Braking components such as vacuum cylinders, air brake cylinders, air tanks and distributors
- Airbrake and vacuum brake pipes
- Etched-brass tank wagon walkways
- Cosmetic coupling hooks

- Cast metal representations of ratchet tensioners
- Etched-brass axle guards, either compensated or fixed
- A variety of pinpoint bearings
- Wheels
- Disc brake inserts for wheels
- Suspension spring details
- Axleboxes
- Brass 0.45mm handrail wire
- Clasp brake shoes
- Transfers
- Paints
- Weathering products
- Couplings

All of these items will crop up throughout the following pages. Before you undertake a project using some of the wonderful detailing parts to enhance and customise your wagons, it is useful to undertake a little bit of research to ensure that you get the main details of the wagon correct.

Research

When deciding upon those models that you would need to collect to represent your chosen time period and operating company fleet, research can be divided into several areas. Firstly, obtain catalogues from the mainstream manufacturers, to see what type of wagons are on offer, to see if they match what has been observed from the lineside. Make a follow-up trip to a local model shop to examine each model, to determine if they are produced to the standard that you require in terms of detail and finish. It is also worth visiting a local model railway exhibition to do the same thing and talk to other modellers about their experiences of using those models at the same time. Research into models does not end there. A visit to an exhibition with a reputation for smaller, more specialised traders offers the opportunity to investigate the kits, detailing components and finishing products that could be used to put your chosen fleet of models together. A combination of ready-to-run models and kit-built items will make your collection

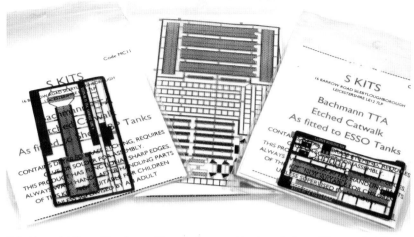

Etched-brass details provide refinement to ready-to-run models where plastic mouldings may lack the subtlety of the full-size wagon. Tank wagon roof walkways and ladders are a very good example of the use of etched-brass where an instant improvement in appearance is brought about with very little effort.

Conversion techniques open up a whole host of opportunity for modelling different types of wagon using off-the-shelf models as a starting point. This picture shows end castings used on a Bachmann TEA model to create a 'lagged' tank wagon. When combined with etched walkways, the completed model will look quite different from the original - and different from everyone else's too!

look carefully considered and customised rather than just a selection of identical out-of-the-box models.

The second area of research should be made on the prototype itself. Whilst books are invaluable, a thorough trawl through railway photography websites and private websites published by railway modellers will often turn up images and information that you will need to determine if your chosen models are

appropriate, and indeed, authentic because, in the past, the mainstream manufacturers have been known to release items that are 'freelance' in concept. Private modellers' sites may give you ideas on how to use detailing components and the inspiration to push you headlong into an interesting project. This combination of model and prototype research, together with seeking advice and knowledge from fellow modellers

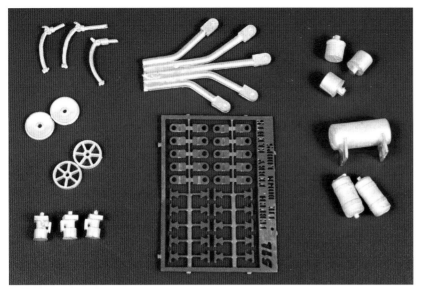

Many off-the-shelf models lack basic underframe detail for braking equipment and other small details. This shows a selection of parts available from a variety of producers including Shawplan Models, S Kits and 51L Models. From top left is presented cast metal air brake pipes, hand brake wheels, ferry hooks and air cylinders. From the bottom is presented air brake distributors to the left and various air tanks on the right.

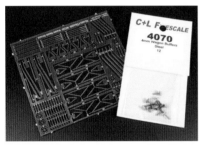

Enhancement comes from surprising places: This etch of superb underframe parts suitable for all sorts of off-the-shelf models is produced by Mainly Trains. The steel buffer heads are by C&L Finescale and are ideal for replacing poorly defined plastic ones on many models.

should be sufficient to get you on your way to building a convincing fleet. Do try and avoid modelling from other people's models because you may end up duplicating avoidable mistakes. Model from the prototype, but do not hesitate to adopt best practices and techniques used by other modellers to achieve your goal.

Finally, when undertaking research, look for those opportunities where the parts of one ready-to-run model can be mated with the parts of another to create a completely different type of wagon. A really good example of this is using the underframe from the Bachmann SSA scrap metal wagon with the body from its Railtrack PNA wagon to create a different version of the PNA. More on that later!

Tools

Fortunately, those workbench tools required for working with ready-to-run models only need to be simple and can be collected together at relatively low cost. Experienced modellers will already have an established collection of tools which they will be comfortable with. Understanding the limitations of hand tools will help prevent accidents and problems during modelling. The following should assist newcomers to the hobby in assembling a useful tool box that will help undertake all of the techniques described in this book.

- Modelling knives may seem like an obvious choice for the workbench, they come in a variety of shapes and sizes but not all of them are suitable for fine detailing work. I use two types of modelling knife: the classic Swan Morton No.3 and No.4 scalpel handles and No.10 and No.23 blades respectively for each handle for fine cutting and paring work. The second choice is a standard No.5 modelling

knife handle and associated blades for heavier duty work. These are also designed with a fitting that will accept a razor saw blade. They are normally sold under the 'Model Craft' or 'Expo' label.

- Cutting mats will protect the table top from sharp modelling knives and scalpel blades. They are self-healing and soft enough to protect the knife blade from becoming dulled too quickly. However, they will not survive abuse such as heat from soldering irons and cuts from razor saws.

- HSS drills are essential for drilling small accurate holes in plastic and metal; including fitting handrails made from brass wire or to open out axle boxes. They can be bought individually or as a pack ranging from 0.3mm to 1.6mm in diameter. The important sizes include 0.3mm, 0.45mm, 0.5mm, 0.6mm, 0.9mm, 1.0mm and 2.0mm. The 2.0mm size is particularly important when drilling out axleboxes to accept pinpoint bearings.

- Pin vices are tools designed to hold small HSS drill bits. They are used to hand-drill tiny holes and are very useful for slow considered work where accuracy is important. Pin vices are often preferred over powered mini drills which may be too fast for good control and also cause friction heat build up which can melt plastic. When purchasing a pin vice, take care to select those with the correct chuck size for the range of drill sizes likely to be used. Double-ended pin vices are particularly useful in that they provide two chuck sizes in one unit.

- Files are universally useful tools to have on the workbench. When it comes to adapting off-the-shelf models, they are used in the preparation of white metal components, removing moulding lines from plastic components and for the removal of unwanted detail when undertaking conversion projects. It is worth having two sets of needle files: one for cleaning white metal components, preferably a set that is not too expensive because white metal soon clogs the files and they may have to be disposed of after a short period of time. A second set of better quality files can be used for filing plastic and they should be reserved for that work, because files clogged with metal will scratch the surface of plastic bodyshells and styrene sheet. Files are graded depending on how coarse or fine a cut that they produce. Sometimes it's worth having a set of files that will remove material quickly to save time and those are called coarse cut files. Those files designed for finishing work are described as fine cut files and they will remove less material and produce a smooth surface finish. Look for files with a safety edge with no cutting teeth. Finally, it's worth mentioning that a wire brush is very good at removing metal filings stuck in file teeth.

- There are other general tools together with bits and bobs that accumulate on the workbench which includes fine nose pliers for holding small components and preparing handrail wire. A set of tweezers is also very useful for obvious reasons! Scissors are required for cutting out transfers, before immersing them in water,

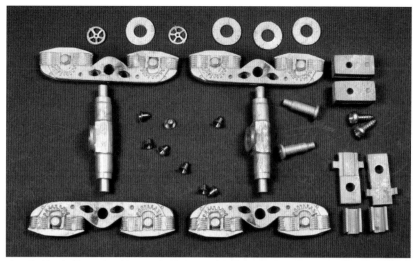

A typical bogie kit cast in white metal. This is a model of a BSC axle motion bogie.

when undertaking finishing work and paint brushes should be to hand for a variety of tasks including painting, the application of solvent cement and the handling of small detailing parts, such as transfers. Over a period of time some items are adapted as scrapers, scribing tools and a whole host of other applications. A fibre glass pencil and similar fibre sticks make short work of removing unwanted plastic detail and are invaluable for burnishing metal before priming and painting.

Materials

- Adhesives are a fairly obvious consumable material to have to hand and different types of adhesive have different applications. Penetrating 'thin' superglue is ideal for certain applications such as bonding ballast weight and 'liquid lead' to the bottom of a wagon. 'Thick' superglue is better suited to detailing work because it is easier to control when compared to the penetrating stuff. Some modelling techniques are better completed with two-part epoxy glue, which takes

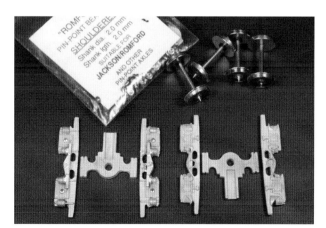

An S Kits cast Y25 bogie kit is shown in this picture with examples of pinpoint bearings and 12mm disc wheels suitable for it.

RIGHT: Using pinpoint bearing cups does much to obtain smooth running and free rolling wagons. A 2mm blind hole about 2.5mm deep is drilled into the bogie side frame and the bearing cup dropped in. A tiny spot of superglue will hold it for enough time to assemble the bogies without losing them.

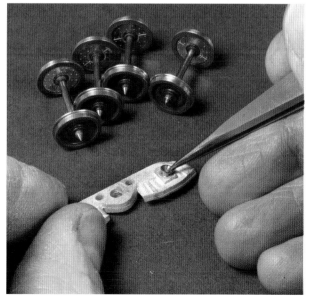

Assembled and ready to go: a BSC Axle Motion bogie is assembled with wheels captive between the side frames. A piece of plate glass is an ideal surface to check the squareness of a bogie assembly.

An assembled set of cast Y25 bogies. Making up bogie kits is a good skill to have because they can be used to make changes to off-the-shelf models such as the Hornby and Bachmann TEA 102t tank wagons, both of which would benefit from the ESC1 bogie kit available from S Kits, for example.

Cast and turned wheels from Markits. The casting process ensures that the detail is retained in the wheel disc. Note the disc brake insert 12mm diameter wheel to the left, for example.

Markits also produces the popular Romford turned brass wheel which is supplied blackened on steel axles. Various length of axle are available. Examples of typical bearings are also shown in this picture. From left to right: waisted bearing, top hat (shouldered) bearing and plain bearing. All have a 2mm axle hole diameter and about 3mm over the flange in the case of the first two.

around five minutes to set (in the case of the 'rapid' types) and up to 24 hours to cure. These are very strong, durable and will act as a filler in certain situations. Finally, given that ready-to-run wagons are composed of plastic, solvent cement has a role to play in applying plastic components and details made from styrene card and strip. One of the problems of using solvent cement is that it is easily spilt but that can be prevented by placing the bottle in a larger plastic container with a small amount of sand at the bottom to keep it stable. The paint brush used to apply solvent cement to a work piece should be devoted to that task alone because once it has been used for this job it is no longer suitable for painting.

- Filler is available in a variety of forms and that includes putty filler such as 'Squadron' and two-part epoxy fillers such as 'Milliput'. 'Milliput' takes some time to harden and cure but is very durable, can be filed and used to make components if so desired. Putty filler such as 'Squadron' takes less time to harden but are softer and not as durable as epoxy fillers.

- Primer is used to prepare metal components such as white metal buffers, detailing parts and etched-brass axle guards for painting, to ensure that the top coat of paint adheres to the metal as efficiently as possible. This is particularly important on parts of the model which could be exposed to rubbing, such as the edges of buffers and on the underframe, especially if the models are transported for use on exhibition layouts. This effect is called 'silvering' and can spoil the overall appearance of an otherwise excellent model.

- Model or clock oil is used to lubricate the bearings on a wagon to keep it free rolling.

- Styrene sheet and strip material is invaluable for making small detail changes to wagons such as adding strapping detail, plywood sheeting

and a whole host of other small modifications that will do much to customise a model.

- Finishing paper such as wet and dry paper is invaluable for final finishing where a smooth finish is important and to be sure that all traces of unwanted moulded detail will not be seen through a coat of paint. Grade 800 paper is a good grade to start with and can be followed up with grade 1200 paper for a smooth finish.

Wheels and couplings

For OO gauge modelling, the majority of off-the-shelf models come with adequate RP25/100 wheels which roll smoothly and will be reasonably concentric. Sometimes, there is a need to switch wheelsets for more realistic wheels with specific detail or modelling in the closer to scale gauges such as EM and P4. There are a number of factors that need to be taken into consideration when changing the wheels on off-the-shelf models. Firstly, it may be beneficial to drill out the axleboxes to approximately 2.5mm in depth and insert pinpoint bearings, either the top hat type or, if space is critical, the shortened 'waisted' bearing. Pinpoint bearings are generally 2mm in diameter and this is why having a 2mm drill in your tool collection is important.

Some manufacturers have produced models in the past where the inside distance between the bogie frames and axleguards is not sufficient to accommodate what is regarded as a standard pinpoint axle length of 26mm. Fortunately, it is possible to buy wheel sets with pinpoint axle lengths of 25.5mm and as little as 24.5mm. This generally does not cause a problem when modelling in OO and possibly EM. P4 gauge modellers are presented with more of a challenge and they will have to look at alternative methods of fitting wheels such as the use of etched-brass axle guards or doing a considerable amount of filing to remove material from the inside surfaces of bogie sideframes and axleguards before fitting pinpoint bearings, because such wagon models will not have sufficient room between the frames to accommodate the wider gauge. Particular problems have been encountered with the former Lima range where the axle length has been as little as 24.5mm and some of the Hornby range where an axle length of 25.5mm is the longest that will fit. To be sure, when removing the factory-fitted wheel, measure the axle length before choosing replacement wheel sets.

Couplings are also a bit of an issue for many modellers. Many new releases in recent years have been equipped with NEM coupling pockets, some of which have not been fitted to the correct MOROP NEM specification resulting in a coupling box either too high or too low. There is much more detail on the use of NEM coupling boxes later in the book, and why the correct height is so important. If you wish to retain the tension lock couplings fitted to wagons, this need not concern you. Also, if tension lock couplings are to be removed and replaced with scale couplings such as Instanter couplings, again, the height of coupling boxes will not be relevant. Fortunately, for those modellers who do not wish to use the original tension lock couplings, it is possible to choose from a variety of scale coupling kits for screw, three-link and 'Instanter' couplings. Those modellers wishing to enjoy the benefits of automatic couplings also have a wide choice and for D&E modelling, the Kadee coupler is growing in popularity.

Moving on

The next few chapters of the book look at various popular ready-to-run models with ideas on detailing, conversion and finishing, starting with the perennially useful Hornby PCA depressed centre tank wagon. It has to be pointed out that not all of the available models can be featured in these pages, but the techniques will be applicable to most, if not all, ready-to-run models. Here's to an enjoyable few hours at the work bench, creating some unique wagon models!

Scale couplings are available under a variety of labels including Markits, Smiths/W&T and Roger Smith. They include 'Instanter', three-link and screw couplings. Some are heavy duty and others described as cosmetic.

Useful addresses
Manufacturers
Parkside Dundas
Millie Street, Kirkcaldy, Fife KY1 2NL
Tel: 01592 640896
www.parksidedundas.co.uk

S Kits
16 Barrow Road, Sileby, Loughborough, Leicestershire LE12 7LP
Mail order only.

Genesis Kits
Waveney Cottage, Willingham Road, Market Rasen, Lincolnshire LN8 3DN
Tel: 01673 843236
www.waveneycottage.co.uk

Cambrian Models
Office 8, 65-81 Winchelsea Road, Rye TN31 7EL
www.cambrianmodels.co.uk

Fox Transfers
4 Hill Lane Close, Markfield Industrial Estate, Markfield, Leicestershire LE67 9PN
Tel: 01530 242801
www.fox-transfers.co.uk

Inter-City Models
9-10 Celtic House, Harbour Head, Porthleven, Cornwall
TR13 9JY
Tel: 01326 569200
www.intercitymodels.com

Hurst Models
PO Box 158, Newton Le Willows
WA12 0WW
www.hurstmodels.co.uk

Modelmaster Professional Decals
PO Box 8560, Troon, Scotland
KA10 6WX
Tel: 01292 314458

Specialist vendors
Shawplan Models
2 Upper Dunstead Road, Langley Hill, Nottingham
NG16 4GR
Tel: 01773 718648
www.shawplan.com

Nairnshire Modelling Supplies
PO Box 6078, Nairn IV12 5LF
Tel: 01667 451130
www.nairnshire-modelling-supplies.co.uk

THE PCA FAMILY

Freightliner Heavy Haul took over cement workings from the primary 'Blue Circle' works from August as a part of a ten-year national contract signed in 2000. The flows from Oxwellmains (Dunbar) works to terminals at Uddingston, Inverness and Aberdeen were included in this contract. Shortly after the Freightliner contract commenced, 66 603 visited Inverness on August 21, 2002 and was photographed during unloading at the Millburn Yard terminal.

Making the best of the Hornby and Lima PCA powder tank wagons.

The Hornby PCA is a reasonably good model and is based on the PC009A and PC009C depressed centre (vee tank) bulk powder tank wagon. It provides many opportunities for detailing and conversion work to create different types of PCA wagons. With a useful underframe that can be adapted for other types of wagon, it's a valuable one for wagon enthusiasts to detail and convert to other types. Lima once produced its own version of the same PCA, dressing it in a variety of different liveries including 'Albright & Wilson' green and 'Lever Bros'. purple. The Lima model is no longer available except on the second-hand market. It is

also possible to use the underframe from both models (with modifications) to create the straight barrel 'Metalair' PCA tank cement tanks using a barrel pinched from a Bachmann TTA, detailed with skirts composed of styrene card and etched-brass walkways adapted for those available for TTA tank wagons.

In this chapter, I describe how to upgrade the PCA to the later type of design, PC009E and PC009P using the Hornby model as a basis, which, at the time of writing in 2008, are on 'Blue Circle Cement' traffic, together with conversions to the short-lived EWS CSA and 'Albright & Wilson' chemical powder tank wagons using the Lima model.

Model overview

Both the Hornby and Lima models have been with us for many years, the Hornby one being part of the Dapol range at one time. Both models successfully capture the classic curves of the single compartment depressed centre tank very well with single roof walk, twin filler hatches and side steps to access the hatches. Turning our attention to the underframe, this has a typical stepped solebar with disc brake callipers bearing on only two diagonally opposing wheels on both models – usually the right hand wheel when viewing from the side. This braking arrangement is correct for a PC009A type. The air tank and pipe

Table 1: PCA depressed tank wagons – spotting differences for the modeller:

The following information has been determined by examining a number of photographs of each type. The basic depressed centre wagon is given as design PC009A and all differences in subsequent builds are checked against this diagram. Lima and Hornby both have used the PC009A model as a basis for some of the different diagrams (and liveries) found on the depressed centre 'Presflo' family of wagons. Note that some differences in filler hatch roof walks and underframe equipment exist between the different builds of wagon. The 51t GLW and a wheelbase of 16' (4880mm) is standard for all PC009 types.

Number sequence	Design code(s)	Operator	Details
APCM 9100 – 9394 APCM 9395 - 9399 APCM 9425 - 9434	PC009A/C/G[5]	'Blue Circle'[1]	'Gloucester' floating suspension, two disc brake callipers, brake wheel and single roof walk. Bottom discharge chute.
TRL 9460 – 9475	PC009B	'Ketton Cement'	Outwardly the same as PC009A
PR 9494 – 9499 PR 10125 – 10134	PC009K	'Albright & Wilson'[2]	'Gloucester' floating suspension, disc brakes to all four wheels with callipers fitted to large brackets. For tri-polyphosphate traffic, an additional charge pipe is present in the tank side. Additional roof walks and heavy duty end pipes. Two top filler hatches but no bottom discharge chute.
TRL 10500 - 10521	PC009D	'TRL' ('Castle Cement')	Outwardly the same as PC009A except for BSC friction pedestal suspension.
TRL 10522 - 10533	PC009F	'Lever Bros', 'Albright & Wilson'[3]	BSC friction pedestal suspension and clasp brakes. Brake hand wheel replaced by a brake lever with the pipe run modified to suit. 'Albright & Wilson' wagons fitted with additional filler pipe. No bottom discharge chute fitted.
TRL 10534 - 10539	PC009F	Hire vehicles, probably 'Lever Bros'[3]	BSC friction pedestal suspension and clasp brakes. Brake hand wheel replaced by a brake lever with the pipe run modified to suit. Albright & Wilson wagons fitted with additional filler pipe. No bottom discharge chute fitted.
TRL 10540 - 10569	PC009J	'Rockware Glass'[3]	Fitted with four filler hatches and extended walkways to match. 'Gloucester' suspension with clasp brakes and brake lever instead of hand brake wheel. Bottom discharge chute fitted.
BCC 10700 – 10737 BCC 10738 – 10837	PC009E PC009P	'Blue Circle'[4]	Fitted with 'Hermann' aeration equipment. Disc brakes all round with callipers fitted to heavy-duty brackets. Bottom discharge chute fitted.
BCC 10850 – 10942	PC009E PC009P	'Blue Circle'	Disc brakes all round with callipers fitted to heavy-duty brackets. Bottom discharge chute fitted.
BCC 10943 – 10986	PC009H	'Blue Circle'	Underframe fitted with 'Gloucester' suspension and clasp brakes (I believe). Brake lever instead of hand brake wheel. Bottom discharge chute fitted.
BCC 10987	PC009E PC009P	'Blue Circle'	Disc brakes all round with callipers fitted to heavy-duty brackets. Bottom discharge chute fitted.

Note 1: Early PC009A vehicles as represented by the Hornby model - largely stored or out of traffic and scrapped. Some were used as internal user wagons at various works including Weardale works at Eastgate. Some converted for 'British Alcan' as ALCN 11200-211 in 1993 to replace unbraked 'Covhops'.
Note 2: All out of traffic, some were stored out of use at Longport for some time. Five were rehabilitated for use by 'British Alcan' in 2001/2 to design code PC009N, Nos.ALCN11227-11231.
Note 3: Known to be scrapped with underframes re-used, possibly under Railtrack PNA ballast/spoil wagons.
Note 4: PC009E and PC009H wagons currently used. Gaps in number sequences as some wagons have been scrapped. PC009P code allocated following modifications to the original PC009E design.
Note 5: PC009G is documented as APCM 9338.

work is beautifully represented, which goes to prove that mainstream manufacturers can fit the correct modern brake equipment to models. One point regarding the underframe on the Hornby model is the rather strange way in which the suspension units appear to be in a raised position, as if the wagon is empty. This feature has been exaggerated and results in a model that is a few millimetres too high – the axlebox cover is about 11mm from the buffer line instead of roughly 8mm, which is where it should be. This is in direct contrast to the Lima model which appears to ride at the correct height. The height of the Hornby wagon could be reduced by replacing the axle guard and axlebox mouldings with castings from S Kits.

In recent years, one surprise regarding the Hornby version is the use of three-hole disc wheels. The model should, at the very least, have 12mm plain disc wheels and, to be as accurate as possible, fitted with brake discs. All is not lost; OO gauge modellers can fit brake discs to two of the wheels and modify the others to plain disc type if the original wheels are to be retained. The underframe of both models will accept EM and P4 replacement wheels without much modification to the underframe.

The model benefits from some tidying up by paring away the mould lines along the headstocks and the buffer faces. The headstocks do include a coupling hook which could be detailed with a single air brake hose and replacement small diameter 'Oleo' buffers. No NEM coupling pockets are fitted to this model at the time of writing.

Useful materials and components

The following items would suit the following PCA detailing and conversion projects.

- S Kits airbrake components including small air tanks and air brake distributors.
- Clasp brake detail from ABS models.
- Cosmetic axle guard components for both Gloucester Floating Axle suspension and the BSC Friction pedestal type available in plastic from Cambrian Models and in white metal from S Kits.
- Sections of etched walkway detail from various TTA and TEA wagon detailing packs.
- Small diameter Oleo buffers from S Kits.

Table 2: Sample train formation: 6B31 Inverness – Dunbar empties for November 13th 2002.		
Wagon number	**Type**	**Design Code**
BCC 10673	PCA	PC018J
BCC 11004	PCA	PC018J
BCC 10670	PCA	PC018J
BCC 11052	PCA	PC018J
BCC 10740	PCA	PC009P
BCC 10761	PCA	PC009P
BCC 10669	PCA	PC018J
BCC 11002	PCA	PC018J
BCC 10888	PCA	PC009P
BCC 10772	PCA	PC009P
BCC 11001	PCA	PC018J
BCC 10748	PCA	PC018J
BCC 10690	PCA	PC018J
BCC 10682	PCA	PC018J
BCC 10765	PCA	PC009P
BCC 10847	PCA	PC017A
BCC 11007	PCA	PC018J
BCC 10875	PCA	PC009P
BCC 10741	PCA	PC009P
BCC 10747	PCA	PC009P
BCC 10678	PCA	PC018J
BCC 11063	PCA	PC018J
BCC 10753	PCA	PC009P
BCC 11008	PCA	PC018J
BCC 10769	PCA	PC009P
BCC 10806	PCA	PC009P
BCC 11054	PCA	PC018J
BCC 10812	PCA	PC009P
BCC 10805	PCA	PC009P
BCC 10677	PCA	PC018J
BCC 11000	PCA	PC018J

Notes:
Locomotive: Freightliner Class 66, No.66 605 in DRFT pool.
Total train length: 938' equating to 3,752mm in 4mm scale.
The train is almost evenly divided between PC009 and PC018 types: 16 PC018J and 14 PC009P with a single PC017A. Note that the PC009P was originally a PC009E designated wagon.

- 12mm diameter disc wheels, top hat bearings and etched disc brake inserts.
- General modelling materials such as model filler (Milliput), epoxy adhesive, styrene card, brass wire, styrene strip and tube.
- A variety of wagon transfers from Fox Transfers.

Modelling notes on 'Blue Circle' wagons

Few products exist to help the modeller adapt the Hornby PCA to different types. Detailing work is relatively straightforward and in most cases, achieved by changing components on the underframe. Transfers to renumber the models are available from Fox transfers for 'Blue Circle' PCAs including the large black numerals.

Modellers will find 12mm diameter disc wheels to replace the incorrect three-hole disc type fitted by Hornby together with etched brake disc inserts from S Kits. Buffers and brake equipment are correct for PCAs in the main, the modeller has to be observant and use photographs to validate the differences on their chosen prototype. Not all of the tiny differences in detail between some wagons can be accounted for except by examining photographs and drawing comparisons with the model.

Converting PC009A type to the type still in common use, the PC009E (PC009P) is a simple task. Apart from a change of number, the modifications all relate to the underframe and fitting of disc brakes to all wheels. The heavy-duty bracket can be scratch-built from styrene strip and there is sufficient room on the underframe to attach this

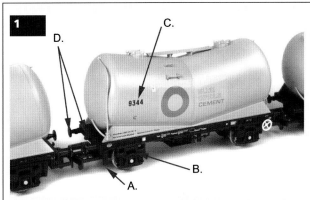

1. The Hornby PCA wagons are to design code PC009A (and I believe PC009C) with disc brake equipment working on one wheel of each axle (A). The model is basically accurate, with correct walkway detail and two loading hatches. It does ride a couple of millimetres too high due to the way the axleguards are represented as an 'empty' wagon (B). The model is usually issued with running numbers which are correct for the design (C). Some refinement can be done to the chassis including removal of a moulding line across the headstocks and buffers (D).

2. The Hornby model features a nicely detailed underframe together with correct airbrake equipment and unloading chute for discharge of the load

between the rails. The modelled suspension is 'Gloucester Floating Axle' suspension whilst the brake equipment is disc braking on opposing wheels, and callipers are located on the right-hand end of the wagon. The left-hand end has no brake calliper. Curiously enough, Hornby fits three-hole disc wheels to its PCA models when strictly speaking they should have disc wheels with a brake disc on one wheel of each axle. The use of three-hole disc wheels is a pity because the wheels themselves are very good quality and would run well on finescale OO gauge track. Modellers can add the brake discs for themselves if desired.

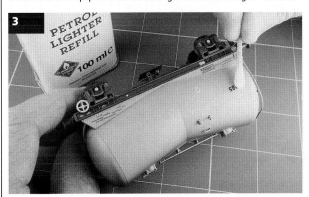

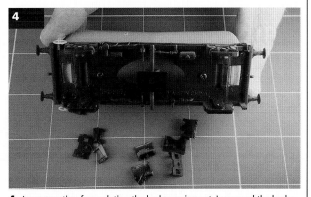

3. Numbers can be removed by rubbing the printed area with 'Ronson' lighter fluid. This removes the varnish finish to reveal a gloss finish underneath, ideal for new transfers. It also affects the weathered finish; so much of the dark grey weathering can be removed at the same time.

4. In preparation for updating the brake equipment, I removed the brake callipers and much of the coupling mounts. I will fit new coupling mounts to accept Kadee No. 5 couplers.

5. The three underframes, with representations of the upgraded brake equipment, to recreate the PC009E or PC009P type. Discs are fitted to all wheels as unlike the PC009A type, the later wagons are fitted with disc brakes all round. Styrene and channel was used to make up the new equipment. Blocks of styrene have been fitted for the mounting of Kadee couplers.

6. New transfers were applied once the original numbers were removed. Weathering

was gently dusted on with an airbrush. New underframe detail was touched in with black paint and then blended in with the rest of the model by gentle weathering. Since this photograph was taken, to complete the model, it has been weathered very sparingly around the roof hatches using matt grey. The grease used to lubricate the filler hatch hinges very quickly discolours to a black grey colour which was dry brushed around the hatches.

7. For the price, these are very good models and little additional detail is required to update the basic model. Hornby could produce the few additional brake mouldings for the PC009P type if it wanted to expand the range of PCAs it offers, probably at little development cost. As supplied, they were spot on regarding numbers and registration plates. As this view of a detailed wagon shows, the models are very good material for quick detailing and weathering projects too.

8. PCA No. BCC10876 is a gently weathered converted Hornby model fitted with Ultrascale wheels and Kadee couplings. Transfers are by

Fox Transfers.

9. The opportunity to add a different type of data panel has been taken with this model of BCC10741.

10. A gentle dusting of cement grey paint together with dry brushing around the hatch hinges completes the weathering of the tank.

11. A 'Metalair' type PCA as used by 'Blue Circle Cement' modelled using a suitably modified PCA underframe and a straight tank barrel taken from a Bachmann TTA petroleum tank wagon. The skirt around the lower part of the tank barrel was added using styrene strip

and the gaps filled with 'Milliput'.

12. Ladder and walkway detail was added to the 'Metalair' PCA using commercial etched parts taken from various sprues of etched walkways intended for TTA and TEA tank wagons.

13. Further variety in the 'Blue Circle' fleet can

be introduced by building the 51L Models kit for the French CFMF-built PCA, of which 'Blue Circle' acquired a fleet of 12wagons in 1980. The building of this kit will be described in more detail in a future book on wagon kit construction.

feature. PC009H wagons are fitted with clasp brakes that can be modelled simply with MJT castings and brass rod. Retain the Gloucester suspension mouldings unless a reduction in the ride height is required.

'Albright & Wilson' PCAs

As my interest in these wagons has increased, I sought out a couple of Lima models of 'Albright & Wilson' tanks that had languished in the loft since their purchase together with a 'Lever Bros' example in a rather fetching shade of purple. Subsequent research indicates that the livery applied to all three models is correct even if the Lima version of design PC009 is not.

I decided to change some details on the 'Alright & Wilson' tanks to represent one each of the two design codes, as far as I could, without having to repaint the wagons. Veridian green paint produced at one time by Phoenix Precision Paints is a colour suitable for touching in details, such as the bottom discharge pipe which is added to the otherwise untouched livery on the tank barrel. To recap: the ready-to-run PCA from Lima

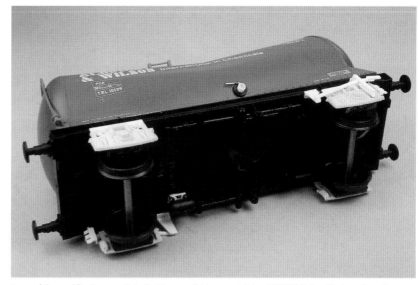

Some of the modifications made to the Lima model to convert it to a PC009F design. The barrel has the number TRL10529, which is useful because this is the number of a PC009F wagon. The suspension units are available as a separate detailing part from Cambrian, or S Kits as a white metal casting. Note the small discharge pipe added to the tank barrel.

is a PC009A design. The 'Albright & Wilson' tanks were built to either PC009F (10522 – 10539) or PC009K (10125 – 10134), neither of which are exactly the same as either the Lima or Hornby model.

To adapt the model to either design type used by 'Albright & Wilson', the

following modifications should be made to the tank barrel:

• Fit two additional walkways located diagonally and adjacent to each filler hatch. I used spare walkways cut to size from a PCA wagon being used for an EWS CSA conversion, drilling new holes in the tank barrel to

Clasp-brake version of Albright & Wilson PCA based on Lima model

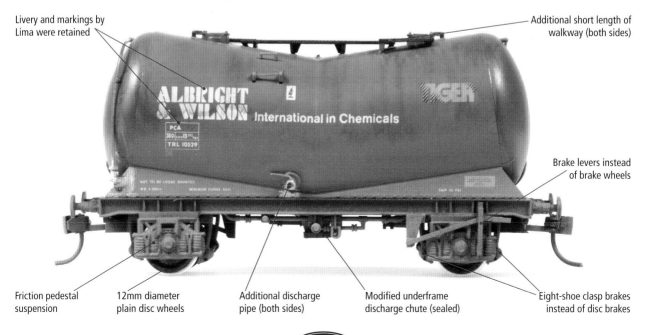

Livery and markings by Lima were retained

Additional short length of walkway (both sides)

Brake levers instead of brake wheels

Friction pedestal suspension

12mm diameter plain disc wheels

Additional discharge pipe (both sides)

Modified underframe discharge chute (sealed)

Eight-shoe clasp brakes instead of disc brakes

PR10126 is a PC009K design with 'Gloucester' floating suspension. This model has been weathered with white adjacent to the loading and discharge pipes. The walkways are taken from other PCA models in the process of other conversions and cut to size to suit the model.

This model represents TRL10529 when complete, modelled as closely as possible to design code PC009F with BSC friction pedestal suspension and clasp brakes. The Lima model (a slightly different coloured one) was modified with axle guard mouldings from Cambrian Models, clasp brake detail from ABS and finished with home made brake levers. The original livery was retained and weathered.

accommodate them.

- A discharge pipe was added at the bottom of the barrel on each side, offset from the crease where both legs of the vee meet.

To obtain the correct underframe for a PC009K type, the following details should be changed:

- Remove the brake callipers from the underframe and assemble new ones from styrene strip, so the underframe has brake calliper brackets adjacent to all four wheels.
- The discharge chute base was removed and the collar glued into place.
- 12mm diameter wheels added with brake discs fitted to all four wheels. OO gauge modellers could use 12mm brake disc wheels from Markits.

The PC009F type has a more complex chassis which proved to be a little more challenging to adapt. Whilst all of the PC009 types share a common underframe of 16' wheelbase, the suspension and brake equipment differs on some wagons. PC009F has BSC Friction Pedestal suspension, clasp brakes and brake levers. The clasp brake shoes were added to the underframe after cutting away some of the plastic at the rear of the suspension units. The front face of the same units was pared back to allow the fitting of friction pedestal suspension units which could be obtained from Cambrian

Models or S Kits without removing the part that contains the axle bearing. This transforms the model instantly. The brake levers were built up from styrene strip and the handbrake wheels removed and stored for future use.

To accommodate the brake lever, the pipe runs were modified to clear the end of the lever itself, this being done by cutting and bending the plastic detail supplied with the model. In the same manner as the PC009K version, the bottom discharge chute was removed and the collar glued into place to secure the detail.

Both models were weathered around the end charge pipes and the new discharge pipe at the base of the tank, but not around the filler hatches. Research indicated that the top hatches are not used. Do not weather the bottom discharge hatch area either. Most of the weathering on these tanks consists of brake dust and rust from the walkways.

EWS CSA Wagons – ex 'Rugby Cement' PCAs to Diagram PC015A

A prototype that attracted a lot of attention were the eight PCA 'Presflo' wagons purchased by EWS and refurbished to new diagram CS003A by WabTec in Doncaster in 1999. They were intended for use on lime traffic between Dowlow Quarry near Buxton and Fifoots

Power Station near Newport. The original wagons were constructed as part of a batch of 15 wagons in 1984-5 by Procor in Wakefield and allocated the design code PC015A and numbered RC10050 – 10064. 'Rugby Cement' was the original owner and operator of this type of 'Presflo', a type that differs from the PC009 depressed centre wagon described above. The underframe is the same length as a PC009 wagon and uses the same 'Gloucester Floating Axle' suspension.

However, PC015 wagons are clasp braked and the tank barrel differs by being a different shape, with a horizontal top and continuous walkway to access a single central loading hatch. Noteworthy was the retention of a vee structure to assist with discharge of the load at the base of the tank barrel. The Hornby PCA wagon is the obvious choice on which to base a conversion but is it a practical proposition? Some detail changes need to be made to the Hornby model to obtain a model that is as close as possible to the prototype, but some compromise is inevitable. One thing I did discover is that this is not a quick project. Much time and effort was expended on achieving a smooth finish on the tank barrel after application of many layers of filler.

The prototype CSA wagons are elusive, as wagons are likely to be when photographs are required. When the operators of Fifoots Point power station went into receivership, the CSA wagons were stored, although all but one have now been returned to traffic. For good images, look no further than Tom Smith's book, *British Railway Air Braked Stock Vol.2*, (published by Cheona Publications in 2003), to be very useful as reference material, making the project a possibility. These wagons were supposed to run in sets of four, so this was to be the minimum number for my project. I saw an opportunity to slot these into spare time between other projects and found

Table 3: EWS CSA wagons:	
PCA numbers	CSA numbers
RC10058	876057
RC10054	876058
RC10056	876059
RC10050	876060
RC10062	876061
RC10063	876062
RC10055	876063
RC10059	876064

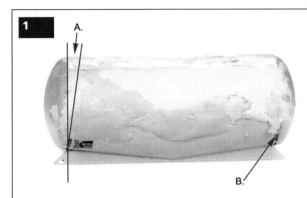

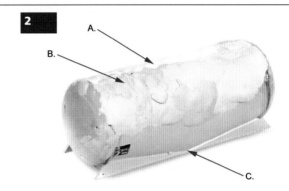

1. Both dished barrel ends are cut from the PCA vee tank and refitted in a vertical position (A) using a two-part epoxy adhesive such as Devcon or Araldite to secure them in place (B). Use the five-minute type to save time.
2. A piece of 40thou styrene measuring 80mm by 5mm is fitted between the end to stabilise them and provide a datum point for filling. (A) I chose to use filler to re-profile the barrel rather than creating a new barrel top from styrene sheet. It has proven to be a viable technique, assisted by the

use of styrene off-cuts glued into place to reduce the amount of filling work. A great deal of left over 'Milliput' has been squeezed and smoothed onto the barrel over a number of days. (B) Rather than apply a large amount in one go, smaller applications make it easier to shape in the new profile whilst avoiding all those strange balls, snakes, snails and other strange creatures often moulded out of left over filler. The original shape is retained at (C).

3. The tank barrel is given a coarse profiling with sandpaper to be sure that the filler is basically even before final finishing with wet and dry paper, commencing with grade 600 and finishing with grade 1200. Take care to retain the crease between the tank halves and not to damage the barrel support frame. It is at this stage that consideration was given to a suitable walkway. The solution presented itself in the shape of a section of TEA tank wagon walkway from S Kits approximately the right length and shape. This picture shows the completed but unpainted tank with

walkways, pipes and hatches fitted.
4. Finished in EWS maroon, the real challenge was finding the correct transfers to finish the model convincingly. A mixture of different sheets from Fox Transfers and City Models was used for TOPS panels, large numbers and other small details. The large numbers came from Fox Transfers sheet F4977/1, originally intended for class 08 shunters. Other items came from sheet F4979/1 and F4979/2.

them an ideal way of using up left over Milliput filler from those other projects, more on this later!

The starting point is to dismantle your Hornby PCA by placing the underframe to one side. A razor saw is used to remove the top loading hatches, these can be stored in the spares box together with the roof walk parts for use on future projects, especially those PC009 variants that have more than two loading hatches ('Rockware Glass'). The barrel ends were removed and glued back in place in an upright position. The flat top of the barrel was achieved with pieces of styrene cut to various lengths to fit between the vee of the tank barrel – the top strip measuring 80mm by 5mm and the in-fill pieces being cut to length to suit. 'Milliput' filler was introduced and smoothed over the barrel, filling in the tip up to the level of the styrene strip. This was followed by an intense filing and sanding job to achieve a smooth, profiled barrel which could be detailed with an etched walkway, end ladder and one of the saved hatches. Care was taken to retain the lover vee profile at the base of the tank barrel.

White primer is used to create the streaks of spilled lime on one model in this picture, a feature of the prototype. Powders can be represented by the dry brushing technique in which the paintbrush is loaded with un-thinned paint and the excess is wiped off with a lint free cloth. The brush is then applied to the model to dry brush the remnants of the paint onto the model where raised detail and other features will capture the colour. Some white was sprayed on too but unfortunately, I applied the paint a little too thick and it spotted a little. This could be corrected with a further thin sprayed application dusted from around 18″.

The chassis was modified by removing the stepped part of the solebar where it meets the headstocks. Disc brake calipers were removed together with the underframe discharge chute. Clasp brake shoes were fitted instead, together with a new air tank and air brake distributor; castings produced by S Kits.

EWS CSA conversion from Hornby PCA wagon in 4mm Scale

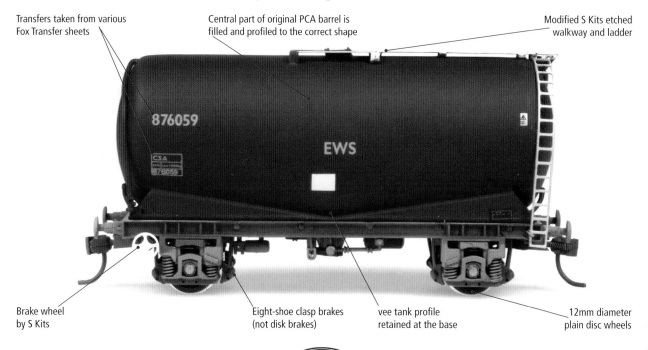

Transfers taken from various Fox Transfer sheets

Central part of original PCA barrel is filled and profiled to the correct shape

Modified S Kits etched walkway and ladder

876059

CSA
876059

EWS

Brake wheel by S Kits

Eight-shoe clasp brakes (not disk brakes)

vee tank profile retained at the base

12mm diameter plain disc wheels

PROTOTYPE INSPIRATION

Freightliner Class 66 No.66 611 is one of the low-geared locomotives used on the heaviest of Freightliner HeavyHaul's trains. 30 to 32 PCA wagons are regarded as the maximum load for the run to Inverness given the two inclines on the Highland Main Line; at Druimuachdar Pass and the other at Slochd. Poor rail conditions during severe Highland weather in winter will challenge Class 66/6s on such heavy trains, although the demand for cement products traditionally drops off during the winter months.

A typical cement train from Dunbar to Inverness is Class 66-hauled and usually consists of around 32 wagons. Freightliner Class 66, 66 607 pauses at Nairn with a train for Inverness Millburn Yard on January 13, 2005.

RIGHT: PCA No. BCC10754 is a typical depressed centre 'Presflo' wagon, this one constructed at Ashford in 1981 to design code PC009E, now PC009P. This wagon has disc brakes that act on all four wheels, which is an advance on the earlier types of vee tank to design code PC009A and PC009C, which have a disc brake bearing on opposite wheels. The wagon number is displayed in large black numbers on the tank side in addition to the TOPS data panel.

BELOW: PCA No. BCC10777 shows a little cement build-up around the top of the tank. This appears light grey when dry but soon looks dark when wet or damp. This is an encrustation type build-up, which can be represented by dry brushing with fairly thick grey paint and weathering powders. It is not uniform in colour, the edges often appear white and variation in colour occurs.

BELOW: The lack of build up of cement around the loading hatches of PCA No. BCC10896 is noteworthy. Anyone who works in the cement or concrete industry will know that strict dust suppression rules are now enforced when loading and discharging road and rail vehicles. As little cement dust will be allowed to escape as is possible, so the chance of build up is much reduced. What is noteworthy is the black around the filler hatches where the hinges and securing screws are greased. That grease very quickly blackens with use and also stains part of the wagon barrel adjacent to the hatches.

ABOVE: PCA No. BCC 10776 shows that there is variety in the position and type of markings together with the TOPS number panel. This wagon shows signs of cement dust weathering. This photograph was taken shortly after it had been unloaded – the suspension springs are not depressed.

RIGHT: Bringing up the rear of an Inverness to Dunbar empty train, PCA No. BCC10812 shows its end detail and tail lamp.

BELOW: BCC PCAs are fitted with 'Instanter' couplings and a single air pipe. Note the heavy duty disc brake calliper mounts and guards seen under the headstocks.

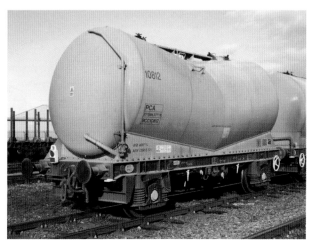

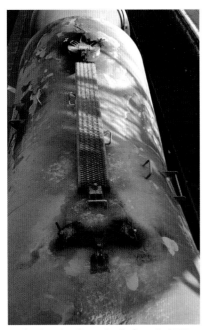

Top hatch and walkway detail of a typical PCA together with weathering effects and grease around the hatches can be seen in this picture taken from the footbridge at Nairn station.

PCA No. BCC10678 is a fine example of the later 'Metalair' type with a straight barrel. There are significant differences in the underframe between this type and the depressed centre types. Not least of them is the difference in wheelbase and overall length of 3″ and the lack of a stepped solebar. The underframe from the Hornby model can be used to model this wagon with some small detail changes and a compromise in the wheelbase length.

PCA No. BCC10681 is a 'Metalair' type with a straight barrel, built in 1984 to design code PC018B, now PC018J.

A variation on the PCA is the 'British Alcan' PCA in the number series BAHS 55531-73 to code PC020A. No. BAHS 55562 is a typical example, it was photographed at Fort William and used on Blyth to Fort William alumina traffic. The underframe is different to the 'Metalair' type used by 'Blue Circle' by having parabolic springs instead of 'Gloucester Floating Axle' suspension, even though the tank gives the wagon an outwardly similar appearance. This would be a challenging wagon to model but could be converted using the Bachmann TTA as a basis for the underframe and tank barrel. Mallaig Junction/Fort William Yard, June 10, 2005.

The former Albright & Wilson PCAs were stored when the traffic between Whitehaven and West Thurrock ceased to run a number of year's ago. Stored and out of use, PCA No.PR9494 is a sorry sight at Longport, seen in faded and weathered condition when photographed in June 2008. It's remarkable that it survived cutting for so long.

HIGH CAPACITY COAL WAGONS

A great deal of coal traffic is centred on the large yards at Toton with frequent departures to power stations along the Trent Valley. EWS Class 66, No.66 095, guides a rake of HTAs from the yard in the direction of Trent Junction on June 3, 2005.

Since the year 2000, high-capacity bogie coal hoppers have become the new 'merry-go-round' wagons (MGR), with several private rail freight companies acquiring large numbers of them to service power station contracts. Not only has the type of wagon used on power station contracts changed over the last ten years but the flows have also changed too, being concentrated on docks that provide import facilities for coal produced in eastern Europe and elsewhere. This means that traditional coal mine to power station flows are not as clear-cut as they used to be as the number of producing mines in the UK, including open cast mines, has been reduced. More coal traffic originates

from ports such as Hull, Hunterston and Immingham than ever before, as low-sulphur coal is imported in ever growing quantities. You are just as likely to observe a large number of large coal trains passing through popular linesiding locations such as Barnetby, running alongside the more traditional freight traffic associated with those areas, which can include large volumes of semi-finished steel, iron ore and petroleum products. Imports of coal through the port at Hunterston now supplements that coal mined from open cast pits in the Ayrshire and Lancashire coal fields, bringing large capacity coal hoppers to routes such as the Glasgow & South Western through Dumfries; and the

Settle & Carlisle line, further adding to this line's renaissance since its reprieve in the 1980s.

On the 4mm scale modelling front, Bachmann has supported the modern freight enthusiasts by offering excellent models of the two most common high capacity coal hopper wagons: the Greenbrier Europe HHA bulk coal hopper wagon, the full-size version of which has been purchased in large numbers by Freightliner Heavy Haul since 2000, and the EWS HTA bogie hopper wagon. Hornby has revitalised its ageing MGR model with a completely new tooling, thus completing the picture up to circa 2004. In the last couple of years, several new versions of the high capacity coal

The Bachmann model of the HTA high capacity bogie coal hopper as constructed by Thrall Europe and used in large numbers by EWS.

hopper have been introduced including the HYA which is operated by First Group/GB Railfreight. This wagon, together with a new version of the Freightliner Heavy Haul bogie hopper, coded HIA remain to be represented in model form at the time of writing.

EWS HTA

In many respects, the HTA coal hopper wagon is a fairly typical modern bogie hopper, with little equipment showing externally. Inclined panels located at each end of the almost streamlined hopper body protect and hide the airbrake and door discharge equipment. You could say that it is quite a boring vehicle to look at other than the interesting shape of the hopper body. Constructed by Thrall Europa at its York works (closed in December 2002) for EWS, a total of 1,144 wagons are known to be in traffic at the time of writing. In fact 1,145 were constructed, however one has already been a collision casualty. Numbered 310000 – 310282 and 310300 – 311161, this is unlikely to be the final total of HTAs ordered by EWS and plans for an additional 900 or more seem to have been circulating for some time.

HTAs share many features common to many of the Thrall Europa wagons in traffic with EWS including Swing Motion bogies. However provision of a fixed knuckle coupling means that

HTAs are usually operated by locomotives fitted with a swing or fixed knuckle coupling such as the Class 66, Class 67 and some specially adapted Class 08 and 09 shunters. This is a departure from the rest of Thrall Europa built wagons which are equipped with swing knuckle couplings enabling operation with any locomotive.

Each HTA has a 75 tonne capacity with a tare of 26.6 tonnes (Bachmann labels the model as a 104 tonne wagon). This outperforms the traditional MGR wagon (tare versus payload) and improves the productivity of MGR style coal trains operated by EWS. Load discharge is also different to the MGR wagon; each of the three clam shell hopper doors are opened and closed by pneumatic rams fed through the second locomotive brake pipe. Each HTA is fitted with two air pipes as a result. The mechanism is manually operated by a control panel consisting of a lock and three levers located at one end of the wagon on each side.

Operations

Class 66 locomotives operate coal trains consisting of HTAs on a day to day basis. Many power stations and loading points are now adapted for operation with HTAs, making the HTA a common sight throughout the country where coal trains operate. Sets of 19 wagons have been recorded in the past,

although I have reports of longer trains on some circuits. They have been observed on the Avonmouth and Didcot circuit and on coal trains to the Aire Valley power stations *via* Knottingley as well as Tyne Yard, Bescot, Millerhill, Warrington and the Trent Valley area. Replacement of MGR wagons has been universal in many areas and enthusiasts should waste no time in photographing the old order.

Example formation from the Avonmouth – Didcot circuit, January 6, 2004:

EWS Class 66, No. 66 094 - 310043, 310532, 310804, 310175, 310469, 310564, 310449, 310324, 310938, 310064, 310325, 310701, 310846, 310320, 311056, 311090, 310219, 310919, 310309, 310413, 310601, 310606, 310605, 310328, 311096.

The model

My first impressions of the model were very positive when I first had the opportunity to review one and that view has not changed. It is interesting to see that good models of modern prototypes can be very attractive in appearance. The livery appears crisp and accurate in application and colour. I found myself desiring a rake of HTAs, some suitable motive power capable of

Bachmann fits its HTA models with its own version of a buckeye coupling which is effective and authentic. There are other coupling options provided with this model.

hauling a rake of wagons that weigh 158grammes individually and a layout big enough for a train of 19 or so. The arrival of the Bachmann Class 66 made the HTA a very desirable model. Here is an overview of its main features:

- **Hopper:** The angles and clean lines of the hopper are accurate and look very good. It is a separate moulding that is secured to the underframe with four small screws. I prefer to see models held together with screws rather than plastic body clips that are often none too secure. The hopper dividing panels have the curved shape of the prototype, but there are some moulding marks in the bottom of the hopper.

- **Underframe:** The underframe consists of the lower part of the hopper, discharge chutes and the main chassis of the wagon. It is crisply tooled except at one point where the join between hopper body and underframe is ragged. Many individual parts are fitted including discharge doors, pipe runs, the brake wheels and label clip. Missing is the uncoupling mechanism rods from the headstocks.

- **Bogies:** Bachmann has tooled a very nice model of the 'National Swing Motion' bogie and have used it on the HTA model as well as the BYA and BRA steel carriers. The internal distance between the sideframes is more than sufficient to accept EM and P4 wheels. The wheels provided by Bachmann are 12mm in diameter with a back-to-back of 14.5mm and the brake blocks line up with the wheels.

- **Couplings:** The centre-line of the coupling is 12mm from the rail, approximately 3mm greater than the operational height of 'Kadee' couplings, in the same manner as the BYA/BRA models. Whilst the model is 'scale' in this respect, it has caused consternation amongst modellers and much criticism has resulted. The bogies are fitted with NEM coupler pockets enabling simple conversion with the tension lock couplings supplied with the model or 'Kadee' No.17 couplings which simply plug in.

- **Livery application:** The quality of the livery application, accuracy of the colours and the care taken to ensure that the livery is sharp gives this model a quality feel about it. One omission from the original release of the model was the wagon number, which should be applied as black numerals to the top panel of the hopper, at the left end of each side. The most recent releases have this feature. The overall finish is a dull satin, almost matt effect which has taken subtle (and not so subtle weathering) quite well. Markings are reasonably sharp and the paint is dense without being heavy or thick. The data panels and discharge instructions are easily legible.

- **Performance:** Without a rake of these wagons and a layout large enough to run them, determining the performance is difficult. The single sample I purchased ran up and down my test track with no discernible sign of wobble. The 158g total weight should ensure good road-holding, even if it may prove to be a tad heavy for some layouts if run in sizeable rakes.

- **Packaging:** Just a word on packaging. The model is supplied in a clear plastic inner carton which is 'handed'. Try and place your model into the carton the wrong way round and you may damage the bar detail on the underframe on a part of the carton that is raised in the middle.

The underframe consists of the lower part of the hopper, discharge chutes and the main chassis of the wagon. It is crisply tooled except at one point where the join between hopper body and underframe is ragged. Many individual parts are fitted including discharge doors, pipe runs, the brake wheels and label clip.

Making enhancements to the HTA

Some new models require little in the way of detail enhancement, leaving us free to concentrate on renumbering and weathering of individual models to add character and reduce the impact of a brightly coloured livery. The HTA is no different in this respect, which is a relief if you need to introduce a rake or two to your layout. Simple weathering can be done in a single session lasting a couple of hours; a pleasant evenings work. Changes to the livery using transfers or the application of graffiti will take more than one modelling session. Either way the end result should be a model that is quite unique to you but without the need for a time-consuming custom repaint.

To change the identity of individual HTAs is straightforward and should be undertaken before completing any weathering. Fox Transfers offers five individual packs of transfers (F4979/21 series) that enables the re-numbering of the model without the need for repainting. Four of the sheets in this series include individual data panels that have separate running numbers that can be used to change the identity of your models without the need to select and apply tiny individual figures. If, like me, you find it almost impossible to get a row of figures even and straight, this feature comes as a relief.

Graffiti is a common sight on HTAs and whilst undesirable in the real world, can be used to add character to off-the-shelf models. Unfortunately I have been unable to locate good transfers for graffiti produced by a UK company. Modellers have to resort to graffiti waterslide transfers from Blair Line (www.blairline.com) or Microscale which can be difficult to obtain in the UK but are perfect for this application. The graffiti transfers will adhere to the factory finish applied by Bachmann. It is recommended that the transfers are treated with Microscale setting solutions to obtain the best results. Leave them to dry for at least 12 hours before applying a protective coat of matt varnish. The varnish will protect the transfers from the weathering process which has to be the most enjoyable and potentially messy job of all.

My personal preferences in weathering materials has migrated from the sole use of paint, especially enamel paints, and now includes pastel chalks. Paint still has an important part to play, especially when diluted to create some effective colour washes. Pastel chalks can be used

1. Transfers for graffiti and number sets are first applied to the model before it is weathered. Transfers should be left to dry for at least 12 hours and subsequently protected with a coat of

matt varnish.
2. Charcoal black pastel chalk is prepared by scraping the pastel stick with a scalpel blade to create a powder.

3. Vallejo acrylic matt varnish from the Model Air range is added to the same container that holds the powdered pastel chalk. These will be mixed together to varying degrees depending on the desired effect.

4. A brush can be used to mix the acrylic varnish and pastel chalk together. The same brush can be used for application of weathering to the model. It is sometimes useful to have a second brush at hand to transfer dry pastel chalk to the model to simulate accumulated coal dust. Paintbrushes can be cleaned with water.

5. A piece of foam sponge can be used to apply the varnish and chalk mixture to the model using a dabbing motion if strong streaking is not desired. It can also be used to introduce streaking to the sides of the model. One major benefit of sponge application of weathering is speed!

6. One method for creating coal dust accumulation is to apply acrylic matt varnish directly to the surface of the model using a clean piece of sponge and then applying dry pastel chalk with a second, dry piece of sponge. The effect can be seen along the top edge of the hopper in this view.

7. A gentle dusting of track colour is applied to the underframe and bogies of the wagon. The wheel centres are painted with a mixture of dark rust and dark grey paint to tone them down.

8. Internal hopper bracing has a trace of dull silver applied to the upper edges to represent where the abrasive action of coal loading has prevented the build up of coal dust and rust.

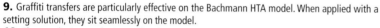
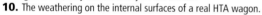

9. Graffiti transfers are particularly effective on the Bachmann HTA model. When applied with a setting solution, they sit seamlessly on the model.
10. The weathering on the internal surfaces of a real HTA wagon.

to simulate coal build-up and spillage on flat surfaces of the wagon when used in combination with acrylic matt varnish. Coal dust gets everywhere and sticks to the inside surfaces of hoppers and external surfaces where rainwater streaks and smudges it.

Past experiments with pastel chalks have proved to be relatively unsuccessful. Whilst they give the right appearance when used for weathering and distressing, unless a final coat of varnish was applied to the model, the chalks easily rubbed off. A coat of varnish often reduced the impact of the weathering effect. Recently I have experimented with Vallejo acrylic varnish and rubbing alcohol as an application medium with great success. The pastel chalk adheres to the model and is not easily rubbed off. It can be worked into seams and around raised detail. I have also experimented with the

use of sponge to apply pastels to the model to create the encrusted effect of coal dust accumulation.

Before you attempt any new technique it is worth experimenting on scrap styrene or any old bodyshell (spares can often be purchased for a few pounds each) before attempting work on an expensive model. Eventually you have to take a deep breath and go for it!

Freightliner HHA

The 4mm scale model was released in the spring of 2007, two different versions being offered: the earlier version with a hinged end door located in the sloping end panel that protects the brake equipment at the ends of the wagon and the later sliding door version. There are some other minor detail differences between these two versions and the Bachmann model has accommodated

these which should satisfy the most discerning diesel and electric modeller. The HHA will enable modellers to provide some work for their Freightliner Class 66 models, which are offered by Bachmann as three versions, including the low-emission Class 66/9 and as 66 522 with digital sound.

The full-size Greenbrier Europe HHA hopper wagon was constructed in Poland from a specially treated steel that makes it resistant to corrosion and acid damage. Each wagon is capable of carrying between 73 and 74 tonnes of coal with an unladen weight of just 28 tonnes. To reduce wear and tear on the track, the HHA is equipped with low track force TF 25 bogies, which in the case of the hinged door version of the HHA, is equipped with a small brake wheel. Unlike the HTA bulk coal hopper fleet operated by EWS, the Freightliner

A great deal of power station coal traffic originates from the Humberside ports, particularly Immingham where Freightliner operate a regular flow to the Aire Valley power stations using its HHA fleet and Class 66 locomotives. Low emission Class 66, No 66 952, passes Barnetby with a loaded train from Immingham docks. 66 952, a low emission type is available as a 4mm scale model from Bachmann.

fleet is equipped with conventional draw gear and large rectangular buffers at each end – there are no inner or outer wagons in the Freightliner fleet.

The design of this wagon follows conventional open hopper wagon design (aggregate or coal) by having the brake equipment located on the outer ends of the wagon. Clearly, it is very vulnerable in this location, especially if spillage of coal is likely. The ends of the HHA are therefore plated over with thin corrugated metal with either a hinged or a sliding door to facilitate access to the equipment concealed behind. This gives the wagon a very streamlined appearance with little distinguishing detail on the exterior other than the brake wheels, door discharge equipment and the draw gear. On the underside of the wagon are located four discharge openings which are equipped with pairs of clamshell doors. They are

operated with compressed air taken from the braking system and manually controlled through the use of levers located at the extreme right end of the hopper. This equipment has effectively made the use of fully automated unloading systems used with HAA MGRs redundant.

The model

Bachmann continued to excel with its large capacity coal wagon models when it released its

version of the Freightliner 'Heavy Haul' HHA. The model matched the high standard set by the EWS HTA model. Its overall shape and proportions are very convincing, with some good quality tooling and accurate detail. The low track force bogies are also very nicely done and it would be good to see these offered as separate

Bachmann has done an excellent job with the HHA bulk coal hopper, which has accurate dimensions and good proportions. The livery is well applied and reasonably subdued, given that the full-size wagons operate under some fairly harsh conditions, which means that they become weathered very quickly.

Freightliner 'Heavy Haul' HHA No. 370 492 with Freightliner web address.
Sliding end door type.   Bachmann catalogue No. 38-030A, 102t bulk coal wagon.

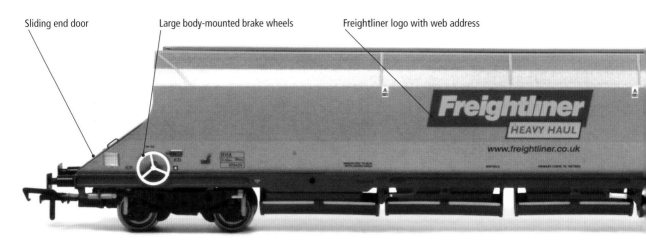

Sliding end door   Large body-mounted brake wheels   Freightliner logo with web address

Freightliner 'Heavy Haul' HHA No. 370 558 with plain logo.
Sliding end door type.   Bachmann catalogue No. 38-030, 102t bulk coal hopper.

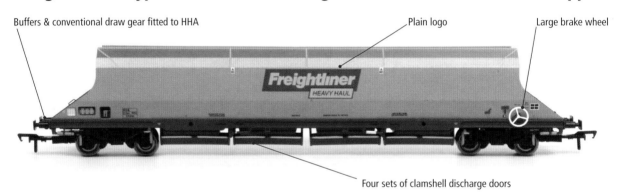

Buffers & conventional draw gear fitted to HHA   Plain logo   Large brake wheel

Four sets of clamshell discharge doors

items in a blister pack so that modellers could use them under other models such as those built from styrene card or kits. In fact this is one area in which

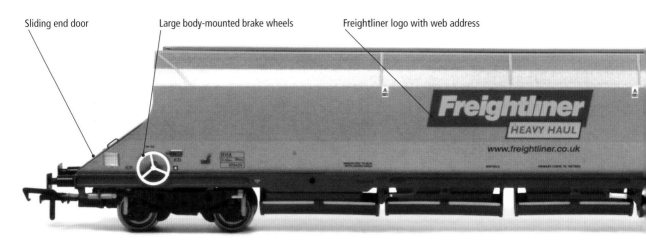

The fit of some of the discharge doors were not particularly well assembled although the detail itself is excellent. Bachmann should be commended on the quality of the low track force bogie that it has tooled for these models.

Bachmann has failed to take advantage: there is a ready market for spare wagon bogies given that it produces some very good models of popular types.

Whilst on the subject of the bogies, they are equipped with NEM coupling pockets which, unfortunately, appear to be slightly too low when compared to the NEM standard.

Each of the review samples were test-fitted with Kadee No. 19 couplers which provided the ideal coupling distance to prevent buffer locking on second radius curves and also offered the opportunity to check the height of the pocket against a Kadee height gauge. Some correction to the height of the coupling was achieved by slipping a small piece of 10thou styrene strip in the pocket to prevent the coupling from drooping down.

In terms of its livery, Bachmann has recreated the Freightliner logo quite well together with the appropriate yellow markings on the hopper and green paint work on the underframe. Given that the model represents an unweathered

Freightliner 'Heavy Haul' HHA end elevation

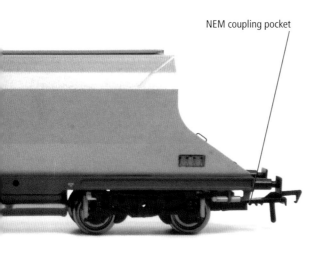

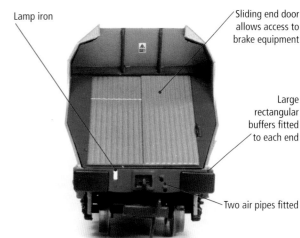

NEM coupling pocket

Lamp iron

Sliding end door allows access to brake equipment

Large rectangular buffers fitted to each end

Two air pipes fitted

version, the hopper has been nicely finished in a dull steel finish. The seam lines on the hopper panels were apparent on the full-size wagons when they were delivered to Freightliner and this particular feature has not been recreated on the model. This would make an interesting detailing exercise with a lining pen and some subtle weathering. As the wagons entered service, they quickly weathered so that the hopper is a dull dark grey colour, concealing any

The hinge door detail as fitted to HHA 370200, a feature changed to a sliding type after the first 250 or so wagons were placed in traffic. Trains are now composed of a random mix of both types of HHA.

Low track force bogie detail as seen on HHA No.370200. This is one of the batch fitted with hinged end doors. Brake wheels are fitted to the bogies and not the wagon hopper which is another identifying feature of the first 250 wagons.

signs of the original seam lines. The weathering effect can be created with very thin washes of dark grey paint, diluted with thinners to around 15:1 thinners to paint. Applied with a broad brush, it will work its way into seam lines and also further dull the livery down. The model is then given a quick dusting with underframe dirt to complete the picture. This technique is demonstrated on Hornby MGR wagons later in this chapter.

Conventional MGR wagons

The first new, super-detailed wagons produced by Hornby arrived in the shape of three hopper wagons derived from the HAA MGR family: the standard HAA, a canopied HBA and the China Clay CDA. They are not new to the range, a reasonable model which was tooled in the 1970s has been part of the range in one form or another for many years. It was tired and in need of replacing with something that reflects modern tooling and production techniques. It is a wise choice, given that many thousands of them existed in various forms (not just the HAA and HBA version) and in a variety of liveries. Trains can consist of up to 42 units, whilst single wagons and

short rakes were commonly moved in mixed trains when the wagons were booked for repair. Wherever you went in the Midlands, South Wales, North East, North West and the central belt of Scotland, a single HAA wagon could be found at the end of a siding awaiting collection for repair. A block train wagon such as this can be used on smaller layouts with a little imagination. The model makes an excellent companion to the Hornby Class 56 and 60, whilst Class 66s can still be seen operating with them at the time of writing. Both Hornby and Bachmann offer Class 66s in their respective ranges. The humble Class 20 also found employment on coal trains consisting of MGR wagons in the 1980s and early 1990s, working in pairs on power station circuits such as that to Ironbridge. Bachmann offers an excellent model of the Class 20 in various forms which could be adapted and repainted accordingly.

The two basic versions of the MGR offered by Hornby as of 2008 include:

32.5t MGR hopper with canopy (HBA)

I am not sure if this earlier canopy type is correct for an HBA. It is a nicely

modelled feature and could be changed to later types by the addition of a plate across each end – suitably weathered in. Modellers should not confuse the HBA TOPS code with the original domestic coal hopper TOPS code – the HBA code is a reuse after the original HBA domestic coal hopper wagons were modified and recoded HEA following re-springing.

32.5t MGR Coal Hopper (HAA)

The standard MGR hopper wagon is faithfully represented without canopy and standard brake gear. This is still the most common of the type in traffic in 2008 and many operate on coal trains originating from Ayr and were recorded working out of Toton too. Despite the introduction of HTAs by EWS, the classic HAA design still sees much use, although many were stored at locations such as Elgin and Perth, being subsequently disposed of in 2007 and 2008 as a return to traffic looked increasingly unlikely.

The model

The underframe is a superb bit of modelling and is accurate except in two areas. The model is fitted with standard OO gauge wheels at 16mm in diameter over the flanges. The depth of the flange means that a compromise in the overall height of the wagon to the tune of 1mm has been made to prevent the wheels from fouling the underside of the underframe. This 1mm has been inserted between axlebox and solebar to create the required clearance. As always, when a dimensional compromise is tooled into a model, other parts are thrown out of position. With an additional 1mm between rail and solebar, the buffers, if correctly positioned, would be too high. Yet they are the correct height from the rail at 14mm. This has been achieved by lowering them by 1mm to compensate and so the horizontal centre line of the buffer is not in alignment with the bottom edge of the solebar. The headstocks are also 1mm deeper. The

Canopied Merry-go-round 2-axle coal hopper. Modelled as HBA 368300

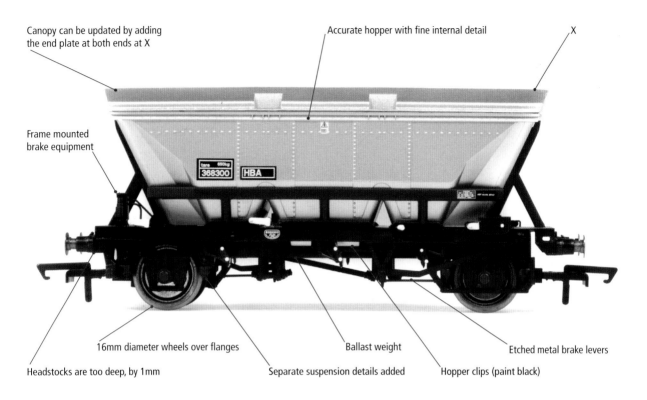

Canopy can be updated by adding the end plate at both ends at X

Accurate hopper with fine internal detail

X

Frame mounted brake equipment

16mm diameter wheels over flanges

Headstocks are too deep, by 1mm

Separate suspension details added

Ballast weight

Hopper clips (paint black)

Etched metal brake levers

Merry-go-round 2-axle coal hopper. Modelled as HAA 355760 by Hornby

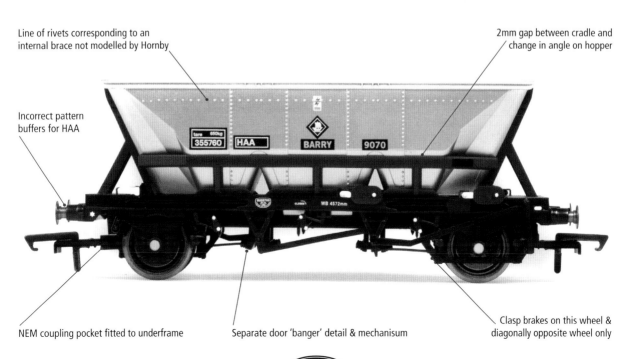

Line of rivets corresponding to an internal brace not modelled by Hornby

2mm gap between cradle and change in angle on hopper

Incorrect pattern buffers for HAA

NEM coupling pocket fitted to underframe

Separate door 'banger' detail & mechanism

Clasp brakes on this wheel & diagonally opposite wheel only

1. The first task is to improve the running by fitting brass cup bearings. The wheels I use for my collection are EM gauge and come with 26mm long pin point axles. Whilst the space between the axle guards is sufficient for EM gauge, there is insufficient room for the axle length. One option would be to choose 25.5mm length axles on the wheelsets or drill the bearing holes out with a 2mm diameter drill as shown here. Try to avoid my particular party

trick, drilling right through the axlebox! Points to note in this picture are the hopper clips which show on the assembled model (A), together with the ugly underframe weight (B).
2. One problem with closer-to-scale wheels is the wheel boss rubbing against the inside face of the axle guard as was the case with the Hornby HAA. Things are opened up a little with a 3mm diameter drill – just a couple of turns is all it takes to clear the boss of the wheel.

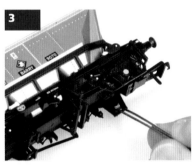

3. Pin point cup bearings are popped into the resulting holes. A spot of super glue holds them in place until the wheels are fitted. This picture shows my preferred type of bearing, the Romford 'top hat' type.

4. Those buffers are not at all right for an HAA wagon. They are composed of a metal turning in a plastic shank. The back of each buffer is snipped off to release the spring before they are pulled free of the model.

5. The old buffers are discarded and the plastic shanks pared away with a modelling knife. New cast metal buffers are fitted as replacements. These are 'Oleo' buffers produced by S Kits.
6. Detailing the Hornby HAA is a straightforward project but makes all the difference to its appearance. Firstly, you could add the strengthening rib along the top edge of

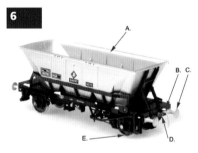

the hopper (refer to the prototype images) which would correspond to the external row of rivets parallel to the top edge (A). Continue with a brake pipe and cover shield (B), 'Oleo' buffers (C), a coupling hook (if not using working 'Instanter' couplings) (D) and finally paint any replacement wheelsets to blend in with the rest of the model (E).

giveaway is the buffer position relative to the solebar.

Noteworthy is the presence of a long ballast weight located down the centre-line of the underframe which is not visible from normal viewing distance, but results in an unprototypical section along the length of the chassis, which prevents the underframe door detail from being modelled. To be reasonable, the ballast weight had to be placed somewhere, although this is seen as a clumsy way of achieving it. Typical weight of an HAA model is 56g and 60g for the HBA.

Otherwise, there is nothing to suggest that this compromise exists on the model. Everything else appears to be correct; wheelbase, solebar, length over buffers and headstocks, width and of course, all those delightful extra details individually fitted including hopper door stop bangers, levers and brake gear. The handbrake levers are superb, being produced in metal rather than plastic. The buffers are sprung but not strictly correct for an MGR wagon, although they are correct for CDA wagons. The photographs accompanying this chapter shows how much better the HAA looks with the correct Oleo buffers.

The superstructure is also good quality, even though the hopper does not sit into the cradle as tightly as it should, by about 2mm. The hopper is a finely tooled model with interior detailing, including separately applied door levers. Internal ribs and braces are represented, together with the hopper door dividers. Some modellers may consider the hopper to be a bit on the chunky side but one thing is for sure, it will not warp over time. Some of the external detail is probably a little more defined than that on the prototype. The HBA canopied version naturally does not show the top edge, this being hidden by the separately moulded canopy.

The pictures on this and the adjacent page show how the Hornby model can be detailed and enhanced with closer to scale wheels and then weathered to 'in service' condition.

7. These models are far too clean. Time to dirty them up a little! The process is quite simple and takes very little time. I always try to avoid over-weathering my models because a light touch is usually more effective, no matter how dirty the prototype. As a guide, I have provided this picture of an HAA taken at Tyne Yard showing where the grime accumulates together with any spilled coal. Note the tide mark on the inside of the hopper.

8. Practice with weathering makes for good results. I could further dirty this model but preferred to keep it fairly understated. There is a

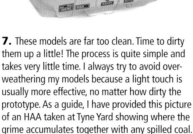

general layer of grime together with the internal tide marks resulting from the loading of the wagon.

9. The hopper is weathered off the model using diluted dark grey paint – some is washed in place, some is stippled on with a brush. I could use several different shades of grey to weather the interior if desired. The exterior wash of grime has highlighted the detail without obscuring it, something I prefer to achieve. The chassis cradle is similarly weathered whilst the rest of the underframe remains to be 'grimed'.

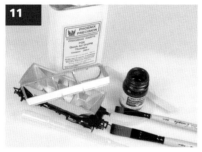

10. Another comparison between weathered and pristine models. The weathering method used on the HTA described earlier in the chapter could be used to add the coal spills to the hopper top using a dry sponging technique and

dark grey weathering powder.

11. The materials used to create the grime effects are shown in this picture. Note the use of broad flat brushes, a simple dish to hold a dilute paint mix and a pipette for measuring out drops

of thinner. The same effect can be created with acrylic paint as well as enamel-based paints.

12. Place a small spot of undiluted paint in the mixing dish. The spot should be no larger than a five pence piece.

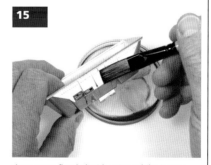

13. The paint is diluted with approximately ten drops of thinners, measured using a pipette. Thoroughly mix the two together.

14. The model is dismantled so that the hopper and chassis may be dealt with separately. This will avoid shadowing of the paint by the hopper

cradle when weathering the hopper.

15. A thin wash of diluted paint is applied with a broad brush in as straight a stroke as possible. Note how the paint collects in seams and other raised detail. Excess paint can be soaked away by applying the corner of a piece of tissue to

those parts flooded with paint. Whilst it may appear that the thinned paint has not affected the bulk of the hopper, it will dull the shiny finish. Subsequent applications of paint will build up the griming effect.

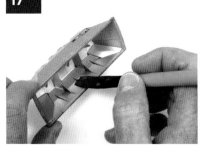

16. The same thin washes of paint are applied to the hopper cradle and the top of the underframe.

17. Once the treated hopper can be handled without leaving fingerprints on the outside surfaces, the interior is also subjected to a wash of grime. It is allowed to collect in corners and along seams. Leave to dry before applying

further washes of paint until the desired effect has been achieved. There is nothing to stop you from using several shades of grey paint to create the desired effect, as long as the paint is diluted approximately with ten drops of thinner to each drop of paint.

18. The typical tide line resulting from the top edge of a coal load can be represented by

stippling with undiluted dark grey paint. This is almost but not quite a dry brushing technique in that the excess was first removed from the brush with a lint free rag. The streaking effect caused by the discharge of the load was done by simply dragging a broad brush loaded with a tiny amount of diluted wash upwards from the bottom of the hopper.

19. Whilst many MGR wagons appear to be heavily weathered, the light touch is often more effective. This view of the completed wagon demonstrates how the silver finish has been toned down and the detail highlighted with washes of dark grey paint. Apart from some minimal detailing of the headstocks, the model is little different to the out-of-the-box product. Weathering was concluded with a light dusting of track colour applied to the underframe. Some additional spilled coal effects could be added if desired and small areas of detail can be spot-painted, including the air hose stop cocks in red and the moving part of the buffer shanks in silver.

The Bachmann 'domestic' coal hopper

There has been a model of the HBA/HEA (360000-361999 with gaps) modern air braked domestic coal hopper available for many years now and it remains a popular model, to the tune of 1mm given that the full size wagons are still in traffic, albeit in limited numbers following the decline in the domestic coal business, operating as HEAs on industrial coal and coke traffic. Bachmann recognised the value of this model since many of the HEAs were converted to various types of box mineral wagon for use on coal traffic, aggregates, ballast and spoil duties together with covered hoppers coded CEA and runners for nuclear flask traffic coded RNA. Bachmann reworked the underframe on its version of the HEA, making much of the detail more refined, improving the running and including NEM coupling pockets. The model now features better brake equipment such as air tanks and a distributor, together with other characteristic details such as Bruninghaus springs.

A Bachmann model of the domestic coal hopper or HEA hopper wagon. EWS has removed the end ladders from many of its HEA wagons.

Like the Hornby MGR model described earlier in the chapter, the Bachmann HEA is such a good model that it can be weathered and placed in use on a layout without further ado! They will accept closer to scale wheels including EM and P4 gauges too. Not all of the various liveries carried by HEAs have been made available and some modellers may take the opportunity to repaint their models to further customise them. Some HEA wagons were placed in scrap metal traffic, which offers the opportunity to model something different. Around 16 wagons remained in this service in 2001, including Nos.360122/259/359/532/627/697/771 and Nos.361092/165/226/240/354/419/467/717/843 according to records, although all but four seem to have disappeared from the records by 2005. Coded HSA, the hopper doors were sealed up and a quantity of non-ferrous ballast placed in the bottom of the hopper to prevent the wagon from being lifted from the rails by magnetic grabs. They soon became very battered, making them stand out from the rest of the fleet. The rusting effects are quite different to the wear and tear found on the HEAs which would be quite interesting to model.

The real story with this wagon type will be covered later on in the book, when we take a look at the various box mineral wagons which have been converted from redundant coal hopper wagons and currently available as off the shelf models by both Hornby and Bachmann.

HEAs have been painted in a variety of liveries in recent years, including EWS maroon, Transrail grey and Mainline Freight blue as represented by this model. They were originally painted in BR bauxite brown (as HBA) and subsequently decorated in the popular Railfreight red and grey scheme which could still be found on some wagons until relatively recently.

ABOVE: EWS HTA coal hoppers are commonly found at Tyne Yard as was the case in July 2006 when a typical example, No.310069 was photographed.

LEFT: A popular location for photographing bulk coal trains is the line between Milford Junction and Ferry Bridge which sees numerous coal trains heading for the large power stations in the Aire Valley. EWS Class 66, No.66 098 heads for Knottingley with a loaded set of HTA wagons on February 5, 2007.

LEFT: Another hub for coal traffic is Toton Yard, because of the Trent and Soar Valley power stations. EWS Class 66, No.66 219 departs the Up yard on February 7, 2007 with a loaded train for Ratcliffe on Soar power station.

BELOW LEFT: The way in which a coal load sits in a wagon is worth noting if you intend to model a loaded train.

BELOW RIGHT: None of the EWS HTA wagon fleet are fitted with conventional draw gear or buffers.

Graffiti is a common problem for the operators but a modelling opportunity for the modeller to add character to ready-to-run models that would otherwise require little in the way of conversion and detailing. Customising models in this manner is one way of making them different to all the others out there! Transfers for graffiti are available from Microscale.

EWS is not the only rail freight company to operate large capacity hopper wagons on coal traffic. Freightliner Heavy Haul has been successful in securing coal contracts in recent years. It has started to use its generic HIA bogie hopper in coal traffic in addition to its bespoke HHA bulk coal hoppers. Class 66, No.66 559 crosses the junction at Milford Junction with 20 new HIA wagons. Unfortunately, the HIA is not currently available in model form.

The dirty condition of the Freightliner heavy haul HHA fleet is apparent by HHA No.370255. The black data panel has been applied to the unpainted steel hoppers which, after a while, makes them very hard to read when the wagon becomes even slightly dirty. This example, equipped with an end sliding door and large brake wheel, was photographed at Barnetby on July 22, 2007.

Another interesting location for coal traffic is Barnetby, located on the bottleneck between Barnetby Junction and Brocklesby Junction. This line sees a great deal of coal traffic for both industrial and power station use. The sidings to the south of the main running lines are used to stable coal trains as was the case on July 22, 2007 when Freightliner Class 66, No.66 510 was photographed leaving for Immingham.

So do you fancy owning some of the superb Bachmann HTA wagons but cannot find the space for a full set? This scene at Milford Junction may provide the answer. A Class 09 shunter moves two HTAs due for repair, as a short train.

A new kid on the block in 2007 was GB Railfreight, who were successful in winning some coal contracts. The wagons were constructed in Eastern Europe and imported through the Channel Tunnel to Willesden, before being placed in traffic. Milford Junction is the location of this photograph of Medite Shipping Company liveried Class 66, No.66 709, taken on July 25, 2007. This particular locomotive has been offered in 4mm scale by Hornby.

ABOVE LEFT: Brand new in 2007 were the First Group/GB Railfreight HYA wagons which are not available in model form at the time of writing.

ABOVE RIGHT: The classic merry-go-round coal hopper wagon is still in traffic in 2008 even though many have been made redundant by the introduction of high capacity coal hoppers. This is a picture of an EWS Class 66 approaching Toton Yard with a typical rake of HAA wagons which was taken on June 3, 2005.

LEFT: HAA No.357043 brings up the rear of an empty coal train at Toton. The weathering shown on this wagon is fairly typical. The yellow painted hopper cradle indicates that this was a Railfreight coal liveried wagon. It was photographed on June 3, 2005.

ABOVE: A typical MGR wagon is represented by HMA No.356917 photographed at Toton on February 7, 2007. The hopper cradle is blue in colour under a layer of coal grime and brake dust. Whilst on the subject of brakes, MGR wagons have a mix of clasp and disc brakes. The wheel nearest the camera has clasp brakes whilst the wheel furthermost from the camera is disc braked. The arrangement of brakes is diagonal on the opposite side of the wagon. Similar-looking wagons will be coded according to braking equipment and permitted maximum operating speeds when empty.

RIGHT: HAA No.356770 sports a hopper cradle painted in EWS maroon indicating that it has seen some workshop attention. It was photographed at Toton on June 3, 2005.

LEFT: HAA No.354461 shows evidence of being loaded at a location which uses tyred wheels to guide the wagon through the loading point. This is visible as two broad parallel stripes of dark grey on the side of the hopper. Other detail to note includes the 'Instanter' coupling, the single air brake hose and 'Oleo' buffers.

PETROLEUM TANK WAGONS

A weekly delivery of fuel and petrol is made to a small terminal at Fort William. The tanks are conveyed on the daily Mossend - Fort William 'Enterprise' service and tripped to the terminal after bogie bolster wagons had been dropped off at the Lochaber aluminium smelter. EWS Class 66, No. 66 110 has six tanks in tow on arrival at Fort William Junction.

An interesting and varied area of wagon modelling exists thanks to the introduction of the Bachmann 45-46 tonne 'monobloc' TTA tank wagon and its larger brother, the 102 tonne TEA bogie tank wagon. Bachmann have further exploited the underframe of the TTA model to produce a variety of different wagons such as re-bodied spoil and ballast wagons, a subject to be covered later in the book, whilst further releases of the Bachmann 102 tonne tank wagons are planned at the time of writing.

Modellers can indulge in a little of this creativity for themselves, as even a fleeting glance through a reference book on modern wagons will reveal a variety of different variations in the tank wagon theme. Commercial realities impose certain restrictions on the mainstream manufacturers in terms of how many variations of a wagon that can be viably produced. Livery changes are an obvious way to gain additional value from the base model. However, in the case of wagons that have had a long life and extended production runs with a number of different builders, it is usually impossible for a model manufacturer to offer every individual variation that can be observed on the prototype.

This is where it is possible to have some fun by customising what is basically an accurate model to create some different wagons unique to your collection. It is possible to introduce variations in the end ladder detail, tank walkways and the underframe by using a variety of different components from etched walkways to different bogies. By the time you have repainted the model and introduced different livery details, it will not look the same as those straight from the box. At the same time you can introduce details that either update the model or take it back to represent the prototype at a particular time. Furthermore, it is possible to convert the basic model to a variety of different tank wagons that carry other commodities such as china clay, bitumen and industrial chemicals.

Also noteworthy is the continued availability of the Hornby 102 tonne tank wagon which is still regarded as a good starting point for many conversions by using etched walkways and other details. It can be purchased very cheaply from second-hand stalls at shows which makes it still popular today. Of lesser interest is the basic and ageing Hornby two-axle tank wagon, even though it has been released in improved liveries in recent years. It has an inaccurate and basic underframe together with some very dubious walkway detail. Nonetheless, it could be used if considerable work was to be put into detailing and conversion. However, to demonstrate what can be achieved in a few hours at the workbench with simple tools and components, the Bachmann models are preferred, at least where the two-axle TTA is concerned.

Bachmann's 45/46 tonne 'monobloc' tank wagon

The model is basically accurate, with many individually fitted details including brake hangars, brake shoes and

Table 1: Bachmann TTA dimensions.			
Prototype	Dimensions	Scale (mm)	Model (mm)
Wheelbase	15'0"	60	60
Length over headstocks	25'8"	102.5	102.5
Extreme height	12'7½"	50.4	50.5
Barrel diameter	8'9¾"	35.2	35.5
Barrel length	24'6½"	98	98
Wheel diameter	3'1"	12	12
Width of chassis	7'2"	28.5	28.1
Hatch diameter	1'9½"	7.2	7.2

discharge pipes. What is noteworthy is the chosen suspension detail, leaf springs have been modelled instead of the more up-to-date Bruninghaus parabolic suspension which was fitted as a replacement on most of the existing wagons in the early 1980s (more or less) to improve the running characteristics of the prototype and is the most common suspension system seen on the surviving fleet today.

Enthusiasts familiar with the basic design will know that variation in detail exists between different construction batches, which can be attributed to the numerous builders of this wagon.

Naturally, choosing a 'typical' wagon upon which to base a model was always going to be difficult. The choice of underframe detail by Bachmann is not necessarily an advantage or disadvantage; purely one of many that could have been used. Modellers who wish to explore different types of tank wagon based on this model should refer to photographs to verify which type of vee-hanger and brake equipment combination they should be modelling. Scanning through my own collection of photographs, I have been able to identify several wagons with this type of underframe, the lack of Bruninghaus

TTA BPO 53774 was stopped for repair when photographed at Fort William on June 24, 2005.

The brake equipment found on BPO 53774 is a close match to the underframe detail on the Bachmann model. This wagon was chosen as one of my projects because it has a different ladder and walkway arrangement. There are other small detail differences which can be modelled too, including the separate hazardous material board.

The air receiving tank is just visible in this view. The access ladder is located at the end to the left of this photograph.

Another opportunity to study the underframe detail of BPO 53774, this time on the opposite side to the previous image. Note the air cylinder and brake lever linkages which are located at the ladder end of the underframe. The access ladder is located at the end to the right of this photograph.

suspension not withstanding. Examples include SUKO 67056 constructed in 1966, PR 58263, a former PR 581xx series tank wagon constructed by Standard Wagon in 1968 and even LPG tanks in the BPO 59xxx number sequence. In all these cases the tanks vary from that modelled by Bachmann.

Whilst the model lacks some refinement, such as the way the tank barrel is composed of three separate sections that do not fit together particularly well, it is fundamentally accurate, which means that it is an excellent foundation for conversion and detailing.

My personal preference is to model a small collection of TTAs in post 1990 condition, particularly those operated by 'Esso' from Fawley and 'Total' from South Humberside. The traffic flows envisaged for my collection include both depot fuel and individual wagons in transit to a contractor for repair. 'Esso'-registered bitumen tank wagons for a Fawley to West Midlands flow are also particularly attractive projects. Bitumen tanks make for an interesting conversion using cast ends and other details for vents and flame tubes. In this chapter I have chosen several different prototypes to produce from the Bachmann model to give the broadest indication of their potential.

Modelling BPO53774

This wagon was constructed in 1965 by Norbitt Pickering of Wishaw for 'Carringtons Fuel Oil' and is designated as a diesel oil tank. Today, the wagon is operated by 'British Petroleum' (BP) from the refinery at Grangemouth in Scotland. It is equipped with Bruninghaus suspension, air brakes, instanter couplings and solid disc wheels. The tank barrel is equipped with a long walkway and twin ladders at the brake cylinder end. The wagon is finished in 'BP' corporate colours but without the 'BP' shield emblem following the re-branding exercise undertaken by the company a few years ago. I chose to model this wagon because Bachmann has already applied this identity to one of its TTA releases. There are clear detail differences between the Bachmann model and the prototype when you examine the accompanying photographs.

Modelling ESSO 56185

A typical gas oil tank wagon in the 'Esso' fleet is represented by ESSO 56185. This wagon was also constructed by Norbitt Pickering in 1965 as part of a large batch of wagons numbered 56000-56199. Although two of the featured wagons were constructed by the same builder at around the same time, there are detail differences between them. This particular wagon has a different end ladder and walkway arrangement to that fitted to the 'BP' wagon. The hazardous materials label is applied directly to the tank barrel instead of on a separate panel. The access ladder is located on the opposite end of the tank in relation to the brake equipment on the underframe. Solid disc wheels and Bruninghaus suspension springs were fitted to this wagon when observed in 2003. Of the two, this was the simplest model to complete.

ESSO 56087 was photographed in the formation of the Fawley – Eastleigh - Tavistock Junction tank train on June 18, 2004.

'Esso'-registered TTA No. ESSO 56138 was photographed in pristine condition at Eastleigh on July 11, 2003.

The end ladder arrangement is different on 'Esso' registered tank wagons in the 56000-56199 number sequence. The majority of wagons in this number sequence are still in traffic operating from the large Fawley refinery in Hampshire. TTA No. ESSO 56185 was photographed at Eastleigh on July 11, 2003.

Modelling materials

To complete the 'BP' tank wagon, I purchased some readily available detailing parts, including an etched-brass walkway and ladder kit from A1 Models, a fret of modern suspension details from Cambrian Models and transfers from Fox Transfers. A close colour match to 'BP' green is Southern 'Malachite green' produced by Railmatch. When the model was dismantled, it was necessary to fill the locating holes left in the top of the tank barrel by the removal of the plastic walkway detail. 'Milliput' two-part epoxy

filler is the perfect choice for this job.

When modelling ESSO 56185, I decided to retain the original plastic walkway detail, modifying it to suit the arrangement found on 'Esso' tank wagons, although etched walkway detail from S Kits could also have been used. I purchased etched signal ladder from Model Signal Engineering for use as access ladder, located at one end of the model. Brass handrail wire was used to complete handrails and grab rails on the tank barrel. The same wire was used to enhance the underframe detail of the wagon. Suspension details were also

changed on this model using details from a spare plastic sprue recovered from a Cambrian Models kit. S Kits also offers suspension and axle box detail suitable for updating the underframe.

Two grades of wet and dry paper were used to improve the finish on the tank barrel. Grade 800 paper was first used to remove printed livery details and provide a finish where the filler had been used. Grade 1200 paper was then used for final finishing prior to painting. The following sequence of photographs demonstrate how I tackled each project.

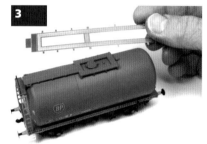

1. A neat and tidy appearance is provided by the new Bachmann TTA tank wagon. On first impressions it lacks the 'wow 'factor but considering that it is a model of a ubiquitous looking vehicle, its very ordinariness is a plus

point. It has been made available in a variety of liveries including 'Total Oil', 'BP' green with aviation fuel markings as a limited edition and 'Esso' colours also as a limited edition.
2. Two crosshead screws are used to secure the

tank barrel to the underframe.
3. The BP diesel oil tank project involves the replacement of the plastic walkway with an extended version in etched-brass.

4. The original plastic walkway is located in the tank barrel with short plastic spigots. They are glued in place which means that gentle pressure is required to break them off without damaging the top of the barrel. Remove the filler hatch first!
5. Several spigot locating holes are moulded in the top of the tank barrel.

They will be visible when the new extended walkway is fitted. A small amount of Milliput filler is applied to each hole and left to harden overnight. The excess filler is pared away with a modelling knife and the remainder is filed back to the surface of the barrel before smoothing down with wet and dry paper.

6

7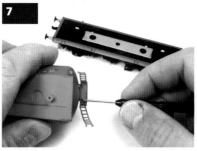

8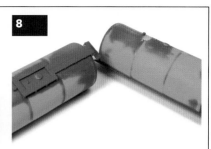

6. In an effort to improve the fit of the barrel sections, Plastic Weld is applied to the join in small quantities. Prototype wagons actually have a welded seam at this point and the modeller could choose to apply fine styrene strip to represent the welded seam. However, the tank barrels are treated to a rubdown with wet

and dry paper after the solvent has done its job. Any seam detail should be applied after finishing with abrasive papers.
7. Turning our attention to the model that will be customised as ESSO 56185, the end ladder was unclipped from the plastic walkway, which was retained.

8. The tank barrels are in the process of finishing before new detail is added. Sometimes it is necessary to apply a second application of filler to the top of the barrel, as seen on the one to the right of the picture, to ensure that an excellent finish is obtained.

9

10

11

9. Both underframes were updated using suspension details taken from a Cambrian Models detailing sprue. The Bruninghaus spring detail was used to replace the moulded leaf springs and the underframe gauged to P4 standards.
10. Conversion to EM and P4 gauges is straightforward with this model. There is

sufficient room between the axleguards to accept standard 26mm axles together with P4 wheels. However, excess movement can be detected when a wheelset is fitted to the underframe, this can be eliminated by fitting top hat bearings. Clasp brake detail is fitted as separate components to the underframe which can be

removed and repositioned so that they will line up with EM and P4 wheelsets.
11. Updating the model includes replacement of the leaf spring suspension detail. A sharp modelling knife makes short work of the leaf springs. Be sure to retain the axleboxes and other important suspension details such as linkages and hangers.

12

13

12. A drop of Plastic Weld is transferred to the model on a paintbrush and used to secure the Bruninghaus parabolic spring detail into place. It fits perfectly!
13. Nearly there - the barrel is test fitted to the underframe. This is the 'Esso' tank wagon with modified ladder detail and other small detail changes, including the removal of the middle rung from the underframe footsteps. Changes are identified with the following letters:

A: The plastic walkway was retained, although the S Kits version could also be used.
B: Grab rails are added using 0.45mm brass wire.
C: An etched-brass ladder further refines the model.
D: Etched-brass grab rails are added to the tank barrel.
E: Bruninghaus spring detail updates the suspension.
F: The metal buffers supplied with the model were retained.

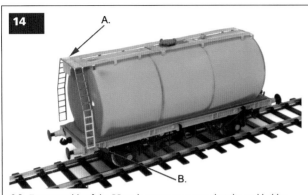

14.

A.

B.

15.

14. Test assembly of the BP tank wagon to ensure that the end ladder detail reaches the underframe and can be secured to it. Some work remains to be done to the end ladder including the removal of the number board and the fitting of a small handrail at A. The test assembly demonstrated that the end ladder would reach the required spot on the underframe at B.

15. When finishing the model we can rely on excellent support from Fox

Transfers. A variety of different packs of livery elements are available to finish tank wagons in numerous liveries. An example of what is available shown in this picture including a very useful multi-pack of transfers for data panels, lettering blocks and safety notices that will suit the majority of models. The hazardous materials labels are not of the most up-to-date type, but they could still be used as placeholders or on a model representing an earlier prototype.

Looking a little on the clean side is the completed model of BPO 53774 posing with a Bachmann Class 08 shunter remodelled as 08 905. Weathering will be applied when time permits!

The Esso tank wagon model is shunted by 08 905 during an operating session on my exhibition layout, Platform 4a & 4b. This model of an Esso TTA will be weathered with a mixture of grey and black acrylic paint applied as thin washes to build up layers of weathering.

Class B TTA project – SUKO 63833

'Class B' tank wagons carry heavier 'black' petroleum products such as heating oil, crude oil and bitumen. Some are lagged and coiled such as the SUKO example which makes up our next project. The full-size wagon was photographed at Fort William in July 1993. The conical cladding on this wagon is quite pronounced and modellers will need to add suitable parts and components available from the trade. The Bachmann TTA model can be used as a base model, as before, with additional detailing to achieve the desired result.

The project commences by cutting the dished ends from the tank barrel and pinging off the plastic walkway. This will be replaced by an etched brass one together with an etched ladder. The new tank ends are castings produced by an after-market supplier, Genesis Kits' ends being the ones chosen for this project, although S Kits offer a similar product too.

Another Bachmann TTA faces the chop – literally to create a SUKO Class B tank wagon. At least one reference photograph should be to hand to verify details as far as possible.

Components chosen for the SUKO 63833 project including tank ends, etched walkways and suspension spring detail.

1. After dismantling the base model, a vertical cut is made to remove the dished end.

2. A shallow horizontal cut along the bottom edge of the tank end completes the job. This is repeated for the opposite end of the barrel.

3. As the cut is cleaned up, a casting is checked for size.

4. 'Araldite' or 'Devcon' two-part epoxy glue is ideal for securing the conical end castings in place.
5. The tank barrel is made up of three sections,

which in the case of the earlier version of this model, did not fit at all well. They are glued together and the seams carefully filled to remove traces of the joins.

6. Rubbing down and cleaning up produces a uniform barrel which can be detailed with a brass walkway. A coat of primer and undercoating in black follows.

The completed model with weathering, streaking and oil spills. Detail painting includes the blue disc wheels and yellow axle box covers.

Additional details include replacement suspension springs, air brake pipes and data panels.

Etched-brass walkways are very effective additions to these models, especially when used in combination with etched ladder detail. However, they are easily clogged with paint if too much is applied too quickly!

Many BPO registered TEA tank wagons were painted in 'BP' green following a relaxation of the rules on the colour of 'Class A' tank wagons as represented by this version of the model which is numbered BPO 87887.

Working with the Bachmann 102 tonne TEA bogie tank wagon

The impressive size of the classic 102 tonne TEA tank wagon is well represented by the Bachmann model in 4mm scale, even though the prototype measured by Bachmann during their research may have been a former 'Class B' tank which was de-lagged, hence the slightly narrower tank barrel. It is dressed to represent a 'typical' 'Class A' TEA bogie tank wagon, against a background of a tremendous number of 102 tonne tank wagons constructed during the 1960s, all of which have many small detail differences from batch to batch, due to the different requirements of the various oil distribution companies, together with production from a variety of different builders. Such differences include the number of loading hatches, type of walkway, ladder and end platform arrangements and their bogies. Add the complication which rebuilding and repairs adds to that mix and one can see why reference photographs are so vital!

Like the model of the 45/46 tonne TTA two-axle tank wagon described earlier, Bachmann had a difficult decision to make with respect to choosing a representative model of this type of vehicle and I think they have chosen what is likely to be the one that

SUKO-registered versions of this model are represented by SUKO 87317. The reason for similarities in both the 'BP' and 'Shell' tank wagon fleet is that the two companies once co-operated with distribution networks and wagons were shared. At one time they were branded with both company symbols.

will satisfy most modellers. The BPO 87xxx series are still commonly seen and still in daily use by 'BP' today (many others are used on other flows, sometimes in the ownership of wagon leasing companies such as 'VTG'). 'BP' currently uses this basic type of 'mono-bloc' bogie tank wagon on petroleum traffic originating from the Grangemouth refinery to terminals at Prestwick, Kilmarnock and Dalston (Dalston is located just south of Carlisle), working them alongside its fleet of TTA tank wagons. They do not venture to Fort William or Lairg; those particular flows are dominated by the smaller 'Class A' two-axle TTA.

Sadly, SUKO registered wagons in 'Shell' livery are now rare, although there are a variety of wagons of this basic

type still in use on other flows, such as those operated out of Immingham to various destinations, though their numbers have been decimated by the introduction of new tank wagons, many of which are equipped with specialised bogies designed to minimise wear and tear to the track. The basic livery on the majority of the remainder of these classic wagons is grey, which was the only authorised livery for 'Class A' tank wagons at one time. Many are operating in weathered and scabby versions of 'BP' lined livery, 'Shell' livery and plain 'Class A' grey colour with much weathering, patching and spillage marks - they are rarely repainted! Grey painted 'Class A' tank wagons have red applied to the end portions of their solebars. Theoretically that is, because

The Bachmann 102t TEA tank wagon offers many opportunities for detailing, conversion and customisation. Brass walkway detail from S Kits offer a host of different variations and there are cast ends for creating further types from both Genesis Kits and S Kits.

the accumulation of dirt and brake dust has all but obliterated the red colour on many surviving wagons.

A search on the internet soon reveals that there is a great deal of detail variation in features such as end ladders, hand rails, brake wheels, brake gear, bogies and method of braking (friction tread or disc) all of which would have been difficult for Bachmann to represent on what is an off-the-shelf model, without creating a huge number of different versions. Bachmann has chosen to equip its model with Gloucester Mk.2 bogies, although the BPO version it has represented actually had ESC1 (English Cast Steel) bogies as of 2000. Many tank wagons of this type were equipped with Gloucester Mk. 2 bogies, and bogies are also swapped around too, so it's not strictly an incorrect detail. The model has excellent stand-alone details for the air tank, brake cylinders and brake push rodding, together with tank discharge pipes, brake wheels and a beautifully executed example of the discontinuous, non-load-bearing solebar underframe, which is a characteristic feature of the 'monobloc' bogie tank wagon.

There are a couple of detail discrepancies to report and, choice of bogies aside, the discharge pipes do not have the centrally positioned vertical pipe which would be connected to the underside of the tank barrel so it can be emptied! Consequently, the brake push-rod that would have been routed around the discharge pipe is not strictly correct either. The buffers, or rather the buffer shanks are not convincing when compared to photographs and Bachmann have not used turned metal

for the buffer heads unlike some of its other models. Finally, the short sections of top walkway adjacent to the filler hatches should be set slightly lower than the main sections. However, as you can gather, these are extremely minor issues which can be corrected by the modeller if so desired.

It is fair to say that the real attraction of this model is as a suitable base for a whole host of detailing and conversion projects. For example, the Gloucester bogies could be replaced with ESC1 bogies to introduce some variation. Modellers could revise the end ladder arrangement to a different type using etched-brass ladder. It could be converted to a 'Class B' lagged and coiled version of the wagon. The variety of after-market components and wealth of transfers from various manufacturers means that a modeller could spend hours at the work bench creating all kinds of this type of wagon. The inspirational pictures at the end of this chapter offer a flavour of what can be done. I tackled two different projects for this book: A 'Class A' tank with replacement ESC1 bogies and roof walk together with a 'Class B' rebuilt as a former 'Class B' tank wagon adapted as a lagged resin tank with Gloucester bogies.

Furthermore, this part of the book would not be complete without mentioning the proposed Bachmann 'BP' 'Class B' and similar 'Amoco' wagons which were announced in 2008.

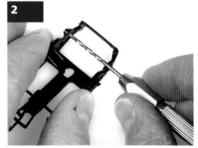

1. The Gloucester Mk.2 bogies are not bad representations of the type. Nonetheless, EM and P4 gauge modellers will find clearances between the side frames to be a little tight and a comfortable fit is unlikely.

2. After removing some plastic from the inside face of the sideframes, EM and P4 wheels will fit. Notably, the operation of the wagon benefits from the use of brass bearings. This picture shows the axle boxes being carefully drilled out to accept top hat bearings.

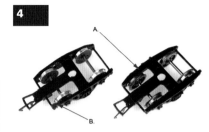

3. Bearings are popped in with tweezers. A spot of glue holds them in place.

4. Quite a bit of plastic was removed to make room for EM wheels. Plastic was removed from (A), taking particular care at the corners so the wheel flanges do not touch (B).

5. The completed job of making room for closer to scale wheels. They are ready for use under the Class B lagged tank wagon dressed as a resin tank.

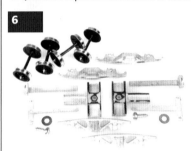

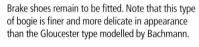

6. A suitable bogie kit for an ESC1 bogie in cast white metal was chosen for the Class A tank project.

7. Assembly is straightforward but does benefit from the use of top hat bearings for smooth running.

8. The ESC1 bogies fitted to the Bachmann model.

Brake shoes remain to be fitted. Note that this type of bogie is finer and more delicate in appearance than the Gloucester type modelled by Bachmann.

9. Further variation on the theme is possible with different cast ends to represent lagged tank wagons. This model was in the process of rebuilding as the resin tank wagon.

10. Replacing the plastic walkways with brass

ones is possible and offers the opportunity to represent different versions of detail and loading hatch arrangement. The incorrect short lengths of walkway can also be corrected at the same time. Those holes will show through the

etches and will need to be filled.

11. Another tank barrel stripped of its detail, to be repainted as a BP Class A tank wagon after remedial work to the barrel ends and top is completed.

12. Filler is applied to the holes in the top and the ugly seam between barrel and dished ends on the first of our two projects.

13. Excess filler is removed with a glass

fibre brush before finishing with wet and dry paper. A coat of plastic primer such as Halfords will give a fine finish for detailing and painting.

14. The Class A tank wagon project with

replacement walkways on a primed barrel. The second project looked very similar to this at this stage. A trip to the paint shop was next, for priming of the etched detail and a coat of light grey paint.

Images of completed model

The completed 'Class A' tank wagon project with light weathering. Further weathering could be dusted along the top of the barrel to further dirty the model because, as the pictures below show, some gain a layer of grime along the upper half of the barrel.

It looks very different to the base model. Those bogies are still missing their brake shoes!

Hornby 102t TEA wagon

This ageing model is still in production and, given its age, offers an alternative to the Bachmann wagon. The walkways should be replaced with etched-brass ones and the position of a seam line in the tank barrel means that some attention will be required to glue it together and fill any resulting seam so it is no longer visible.

The bogies on the Hornby model are a work of fiction and benefit from replacement with ESC1 bogie kits as demonstrated earlier in the chapter. However, it is popular with wagon enthusiasts because of its accurate barrel dimensions which lends it to many conversions including Class B tank wagons with lagging plates and conical tank ends.

The finished resin TEA tank wagon in light grey instead of the usual black reserved for lagged Class B tanks.

RIGHT: The original Bachmann Gloucester bogie fitted with EM wheels.

Reference material

There is a great deal of reference material which I refer to time and again when modelling tank wagons. My favourite magazine article on the subject was written by Paul W. Bartlett, illustrated by Peter Fidczuk and published in the April 1992 issue of *Model Railways* magazine. It is worth making the attempt to obtain a copy of this issue because the scale drawing and photographs used to illustrate the article are very useful.

Metro Enterprises Ltd. published a series of books on private owner wagons, and I refer you to volume two which provides a great deal of both number and constructional data for all privately owned tank wagons 'authorised to run on British Rail'. Andrew Marshall is the author of this particular book.

A long out of print publication but a firm favourite of mine is the comprehensive guide on private owner wagons by David Ratcliffe, *Modern Private Owner Wagons on British Rail*, published by Patrick Stevens Limited in 1989. This has a chapter which describes various petroleum tank wagons together with some excellent photographs.

Finally, I have described the modelling of tank wagons supported by reference photographs in my own book, *Thoroughly Modern Models 2: Modern Wagons in 4mm*, published by Irwell Press.

PROTOTYPE INSPIRATION

Bitumen tank wagons can be modelled from the Bachmann and Hornby TTA models by replacing the dished ends with conical ends and adding small details such as flame tubes and top vents. The consistency of bitumen means that it needs heat to liquefy it for unloading after extended transit times, which accounts for the very distressed appearance of the wagons. The material itself is sticky and spills cling to the barrel, whilst the heat encourages rust and blisters the paint. This wagon is operated by Esso from Fawley and was in transit to Tavistock Junction.

TTA No. BPO 53752 shows off its walkway detail, which can be represented on a model with etched brass fittings. It was constructed by Norbitt-Pickering in 1966 as a kerosene tank for 'Charringtons Fuel Oils Ltd'.

TTA No. BPO 37263 is a diesel tank wagon built by Norbitt-Pickering in 1966. Note that the 'BP' logo has been painted over and it still has a 'Railfreight Petroleum' logo. It was photographed in the consist of a Lairg-Grangemouth working in April 2006.

LEFT: This photograph shows a view of the small terminal at Fort William demonstrating that such facilities do not need to be large. This is an ideal subject for modelling because the storage tanks and road loading bays are behind a screen of trees, out of sight to the left of this picture, on the other side of the line. If space is an issue, modelling of the oil terminal could be avoided without loosing the operating potential.

BELOW: The walkway detail of No. BPO 53774 which was constructed by Norbitt-Pickering in 1966 as a diesel tank for 'Charringtons Fuel Oils Ltd'.

TEA No. BPO 87670 was photographed with a variety of bogie tank wagons at Barnetby in the summer of 2007. It was constructed by Metro Cammell in 1967. Note the use of Gloucester Mk.3 bogies as modelled by Bachmann.

ABOVE: The BRT 84000-41 series of tank wagons were built by Norbitt-Pickering in 1967 and found use on the Port Clarence traffic with 'Phillips Petroleum'. TEA No. BRT 84018 was photographed at Longport when stored out of use. Several details worthy of note include the use of Gloucester bogies, a strengthening bracket above the bogies, walkways that do not extend the full length of the wagon and what appears to be the remains of 'Esso' markings.

BELOW: Stored out of use at Longport in June 2005 was TEA No. BPO 87877, an aviation fuel tank believed to be constructed by Metro Cammell in 1968-9. This wagon was equipped with ESC1 bogies which can be represented using a cast metal kit to replace the Gloucester type modelled by Bachmann.

BALLAST HOPPER WAGONS

Making the best of what are considered some of the very best ready to run UK-outline wagons around.

A long ballast train enters Doncaster Yard from the Worksop direction, hauled by an EWS Class 66, 66 077 *Benjamin Gimbert GC*. The first wagons are HQA bogie ballast hoppers which are similar to the JJA type announced by Bachmann as part of its 2008-9 release programme. The rear of the train is dominated by a mixture of 'Seacows', 'Sealions' and 'Stingrays', which are available from Hornby and Bachmann collectively. Modelling a 'Stingray' requires some work with styrene sheet and plastic rod.

If you surveyed a ballast train of typical 40t 'Seacow'/'Sealion' bogie ballast hoppers today, it is unlikely that any two will be identical in appearance. I examined a train of such wagons in March 2008 at Doncaster (see the picture above), photographing 21 of the hoppers in the train. Not one was the same. The train consisted of a variety of liveries (under the grime), patch painting and fittings for various lighting systems or variations in the canopy. For the modeller, depending on how heavy one likes to apply weathering, a train could be modelled with absolutely no uniformity. Some of the wagons photographed that day are featured at the end of the chapter.

There is one other ready-to-run model to consider and that is the two-axle Heljan 'Dogfish' ballast hopper. Unfortunately, at the time of writing, its smaller cousin, the 'Catfish' was only available to model from a kit. The 'Dogfish' is now rarely seem on Network Rail but the Heljan model is nonetheless as important as the bogie ballast hopper wagons. Before tackling the 'Dogfish', the bogie ballast hoppers will be investigated.

What's available

An examination of the available records reveals the following information on 'Sealion' and 'Seacow' bogie ballast wagons. I have also added details of the

'Walrus' and 'Whale' wagons too, for the sake of a complete set of records, although kit-building and cross-kitting would be necessary to obtain an example.

1. 'Walrus'

Based on the Southern Railway Diagrams 1774 and 1775, 50 'Walrus' were constructed with plate bogies and other detail differences in 1954 by Metro-Cammell of Birmingham. Although regarded as inferior to the original SR design, they did, however, survive for many years and were numbered in the DB9925xx series. It is possible to model this early type by using, and for some cases, modifying a plastic kit produced by Cambrian Models.

When it was first released, the Lima 'Sealion' model was regarded as being particularly good for the UK outline market when compared against other products available to modellers at the time. Hornby have re-tooled the bogies and added refinements in the form of safety canopies.

3. 'Sealion'

They were constructed in batches at Shildon, the first one being Lot 3723 DB982440-982539 as YGH with dual air and AFI braking equipment in 1971. Some have been converted to 'Seacows' by the removal of the AFI equipment and many have lost their vacuum brake pipes (YGB), being coded YGA. Some are equipped with lighting and associated generators, being renamed 'Stingray'. This is the wagon on which the former Lima bogie ballast wagon is based, a model re-issued by Hornby in 2007 with new bogie mouldings and upgraded detail.

4. 'Seacow'

Constructed as YGB at Shildon as Lot 3724 in 1971 as DB982540-564.

5. 'Seacow'

Constructed as YGB at Shildon in 1971 as Lot 3777 as DB982565-567.

6. 'Sealion'/'Seacow'

Constructed at Shildon between 1972 and 1974 as Lot 3802, numbered DB982568-982927. The Bachmann model released in 2007 represents the 1970s design both as a 'Sealion' and a 'Seacow' (with AFI brake equipment removed). The former Lima wagon can be adapted to represent a 'Seacow' by removal of the AFI detail from one end platform.

7. 'Seacow'

In 1981, a modern version of the 'Sealion' design, featuring welded construction and Y27 bogies, was

New bogies and a good, well-researched finish make the former Lima 'Sealion' appear more contemporary in quality. 'Dutch' yellow/grey livery sits well on this model. It is amazing how good printed detail is these days and that alone does much for the finish on models. Repainting becomes unnecessary if you can find the right transfers to renumber the model to suit your collection.

2. 'Whale'

The 'Whale' (YHA) was appropriately named because of its large size and bulk, which did ultimately result in structural problems. Records indicate they were constructed at Shildon in 1966 and 1967 and were numbered DB982350-439.. They were equipped with plate bogies with roller bearings, and despite early problems remained in traffic until around 1998-1999, some were even repainted in 'Dutch' engineers yellow and grey livery. Cambrian Models released a plastic kit for the 'Whale' in 2008, the construction of which is outside the scope of this book.

Table 1: 40 tonne BR bogie ballast wagons represented by off-the-shelf models.				
Fish Type	**Number**	**Builder**	**Date**	**Diagram**
'Sealion' [a]	DB982440 - 982539	BR Shildon	1971	1/590
'Sealion' [a]	DB982568 - 982927	BR Shildon	1972 to 1974	1/590
'Seacow'	DB982540-567	BR Shildon	1971	1/591
'Seacow'	DB980000 - 980244	BR Ashford and Shildon	1981 to 1982	YG500H
'Seacow'	DB980245 - 980250	BR Shildon	1982	
[a] Many 'Sealion' wagons were converted to 'Seacow' by the removal of AFI brake equipment. Some are fitted with lighting.				

constructed at Shildon in 1981-2 (DB980000 to DB980144) and Ashford (DB980145 to DB980244) as Lot 3966, together with a further small batch built at Shildon in 1982 numbered DB980245-250. Coded as a YGB (many are now only equipped with air brakes and coded YGA), this type is represented by the Hornby model. Some are modified with lighting equipment and there are also 'Stingrays' converted from this batch.

With many of the fleet of 'Seacows' and 'Sealions' over 35 years old, many changes have taken place, including changes to brake equipment, the installation of lighting and generators together with repairs and re-plating. Photographs of particular wagons should be sought before starting a project, if modelling specific details are important to you. Reference pictures are provided at the end of the chapter and noteworthy is the poor external condition of some of these wagons today.

As far as the models are concerned, little needs to be done to them other than wagon-specific detailing and conversion because, in the main, both the Hornby and Bachmann 'Seacows' are pretty accurate. The Bachmann model accepts wheels with 26mm long pinpoint axles without difficulty, whilst the Hornby one utilises wheelsets with

Two ballast wagons suitable for up-to-date operations are offered by Bachmann. To the rear of the picture is an EWS YGA with extended safety canopies. In front of that is the YGB BR Departmental version. Bachmann has correctly modelled the interior dividing panel in its ballast wagon. All that remains is some weathering work and patch painting to represent repairs.

25.5mm axles making closer-to-scale conversions more complex. Here is an overview of the available models – we seem to be more than adequately equipped for ballasting the permanent way on our D&E era layouts. A little more work is required on the former Lima 'Sealion', but it too has a place on a contemporary layout.

The Bachmann 'Seacow' (YGA, YGB) and 'Sealion' (YGH)

This model is based on the first 40t ballast hoppers constructed in the 1950s as 'Seacows'. It was released in 2007 as a completely new model. Three

versions make up the first release including an EWS YGA 'Seacow', BR Departmental YGB 'Seacow' and a YGH 'Sealion'. The model represents the original BR-built wagons equipped with Gloucester bogies and of riveted construction. The original 'Sealion' wagons were dual-braked with vacuum AFI and air brake equipment, most of which was mounted on the end platforms. The YGA and YGB versions are only equipped with air brake detail, whilst the BR olive green YGH version features vacuum cylinders, AFI equipment and air brake equipment.

Bachmann has been very careful to equip each wagon with the appropriate

Perhaps my favourite livery is the British Rail departmental (Dutch) livery which sits on the Bachmann model particularly well. The interior is painted pale grey which is best repainted in a dark rust colour before weathering the model.

EWS has removed the through vacuum pipe and associated equipment from many of its 'Seacow' ballast hopper wagons and re-coded them as YGA. This version of the Bachmann model represents the most up-to-date version of the 'Seacow' complete with extended safety canopies.

ABOVE: Whilst there are many delicate-looking parts applied to the new Hornby 'Seacow' model, they are surprisingly robust, particularly the handrails and overhead electrification guards. The underframe details are correctly modelled including the discharge chutes, Y27 bogies and underframe members. It is worth pointing out that no NEM coupling pockets are provided on the Hornby 'Seacow'.

RIGHT: Delicate detailing sets this model apart from the rest of the Hornby range of modern wagons, including the HAA family. Noteworthy is the use of etched mesh for walkways and the overhead electrification guards.

brake equipment and electrification safety canopies at each end of the wagon. For example, the BR olive green 'Sealion' has no canopy at all making it suitable for layouts based on the BR corporate blue and BR green eras. The EWS model represents a bang up-to-date 'Seacow' with extended platform safety canopies.

On a technical front, the Bachmann model features a diecast frame giving the wagon a reasonable operating weight of 82g whilst retaining an empty hopper. It is equipped with NEM coupler pockets set to the specified height. The bogies

Mainline blue is applied to DB980052 together with some superbly printed details. This pristine model is ripe for paint fading and custom weathering work to represent ballast dust, dirt and sun bleaching. Hornby has helped the modeller by painting the hopper interior in a suitable dark rusty oxide brown colour.

are fitted with RP25 profile wheels mounted on 26mm length axles which are a good fit in the bogies, although they benefit further from the use of top hat bearings. The model features a great deal of additional detail fitted as individual components including pipe runs, brake cylinders, and wheels, handrails and platform detail.

The Hornby/Lima 'Sealion'

When it was first released, the Lima 'Sealion' model was regarded as being particularly good for the UK outline market when compared against other

products available to modellers at the time. It has stood the passage of time particularly well and the upgraded version offered by Hornby would pass muster on the majority of layouts using contemporary models produced today. Technically, the model lacks NEM coupling pockets and is devoid of many of the small details present on the Bachmann model. However, upgrading the model included the use of details from the YGB (1981) 'Seacow' model including safety canopies over each platform. Unfortunately, Hornby included the safety platforms on the green version of its 'Sealion' and for the majority of modellers collecting models in that livery, it would be inappropriate. The wheels are fitted to 2mm diameter pinpoint axles of 25.5mm length and are 12.6mm in diameter. It weighs in at 54g.

Noteworthy is the design of the re-tooled bogies which are too narrow for drop-in conversion with closer-to-scale wheels. The axleboxes must be drilled out to accommodate 26mm length axles and, with a mere 27.8mm over the outside of the axle boxes, there will be little room to accommodate suitable bearings as well. Although it is possible to purchase EM gauge wheels with 25.5mm pinpoint axles, there is

Heljan's first foray into ready to run wagons is the ZFV 'Dogfish' ballast wagon and overall it is not such a bad model. However, modellers were surprised to find that HO standard wheels were fitted complete with shortened axles in narrow frames.

little room between the inside of the bogie frames to accommodate those wheels. P4 gauge modellers will struggle unless the bogies are completely rebuilt with new spacers.

The Hornby 1981 'Seacow'

Hornby has chosen to base its 'Seacow' ballast wagon on the modern Diagram YG500H version which was constructed at Ashford and Shildon between 1981 and 1982. It features Y27 bogies, welded bodyside ribs and electrification guards fitted to the end platforms.

The hopper and end platforms are superbly tooled, with crisp detail and accurate dimensions including the complex curves in the hopper interior. The body is enhanced with a tremendous amount of separately applied detail, which is very delicate in appearance and perfectly executed, each item being seamlessly fitted. Even though modellers are becoming more and more accustomed to the use of individual components for the detailing of ready-to-run models, this one is pretty exceptional, especially when you examine the brake equipment on one of the end platforms, which includes delicate pipe runs and an accurately modelled air brake distributor and receiving tank. Each handrail is individually applied too, and although they are very fine, they appear to be surprisingly robust.

The later 1981 to 1982 build of 'Seacow' ballast wagons were fitted with Y27 bogies and Hornby has done a good job of these. Individual brake blocks are modelled and these are in-line with the wheels. It is worth noting that the cosmetic sideframes are moulded fairly close together, the measurements between the inside faces being no more than 21.5mm. EM gauge wheels will fit – just, if used on 25.5mm long axles. P4 modellers will find it a little more challenging to install scale wheels to this model. In any case, modellers that prefer a closer to scale wheels will have to adjust the brake blocks to prevent them running on the wheel flanges.

The Heljan ZFV 'Dogfish'

Sitting on its own in the world of ballast hoppers is Heljan's first wagon model, the 'Dogfish' ballast hopper, which hit the shops in January 2005 and was well received by most modellers. The initial release is of six versions of the model,

Table 2: 'Dogfish' number sequences: 24t ballast hopper wagon to Diagram1/587.		
Number	**Date**	**Builder**
DB983000 - 983309	1957	Chas Roberts
DB983577 - 983626	1960	BR Shildon
DB983897 - 983920	1961	BR Shildon
DB992711 - 992858	1956	Chas Roberts
DB992859 - 993058	1956 and 1957	Metro Cammell
DB993059 - 993148	1956 and 1957	Chas Roberts
DB993149 - 993309	1956 and 1957	Metro Cammell
DB993310 - 993507	1957 and 1958	Metro Cammell
DB993567 - 993634	1960	BR Shildon
Note: Air braked 'Dogfish' are coded HPA with around 57 left in traffic as of 2006.		

three in engineers' olive green and three in engineers Dutch grey and yellow, each with different running numbers. The models are finished to a high standard, including quality printing for number panels and data panels, correct colour rendition and an evenly applied eggshell finish. Unfortunately, there does not appear to be any move to offer a 'Catfish' and modellers are left to construct the Cambrian Models kit if 'Catfish' are desired.

One feature of the model is that HO scale wheels are provided and HO wheels have shorter axles than OO gauge wheelsets. Concern was expressed about the potential difficulty in converting the model to either EM gauge or P4/S4 gauge and it was logical to assume that the axleguards were too close together to accept the finer gauges too. This together with some fairly nondescript detailing of the chassis attracted some criticism. The conversion to closer to scale gauge is not as difficult as once thought and may be completed as part of a general detailing project in a matter of an hour or so. The process is described later in the chapter.

The vacuum braked 'Dogfish' were constructed in several batches and were quite common at one time together with its smaller brother, the 'Catfish'. Today, few 'Dogfish' remain in traffic and are air braked, being retained for more specialised jobs. Their role has been overtaken by a variety of modern wagons including the JJA 'Auto-ballaster', a large bogie wagon which has been proposed by Bachmann as a new 4mm scale model in plastic.

Improving the Bachmann 'Sealion' and 'Seacow' models

1. A small bag of detailing parts is supplied with the Bachmann model for application by the modeller.

2. This view shows the fitting of factory supplied parts to the Bachmann model. It is a simple task to place a spot of superglue on a small scrap of styrene and then apply glue with a cocktail stick to avoid flooding the parts.

3. For some strange reason, Bachmann supplied the first run of its 'Seacow' and 'Sealion' with pale grey interiors. A coat of dark rust soon kills the overly bright appearance and becomes the base coat for weathering effects.

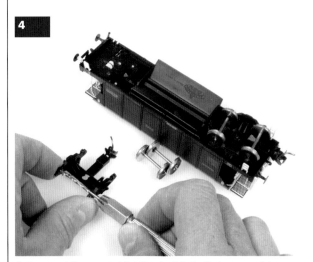

4. Some modellers reported that the wheels in the Bachmann model appeared to be too slack in the bogies. Some wheelsets had dropped out of the bogies before the model was removed from the box. Whilst the axles should be 26mm in length, the space between the sideframes is slightly greater. A simple cure is to fit turned brass pinpoint bearing cups. Open out the

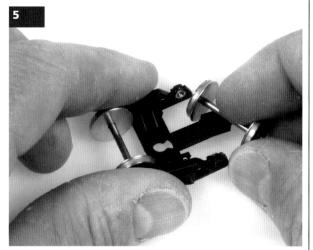

axlebox first using a 2mm diameter drill, without drilling right through!
5. This picture shows the pinpoint bearing cup inserted and new wheels being fitted. They are to EM gauge to suit my layout. There is sufficient room to fit P4 gauge wheels too. The use of the bearings reduces the side-to-side play of the wheels almost to nothing.

Fitting finescale wheels to the Hornby 'Seacow'

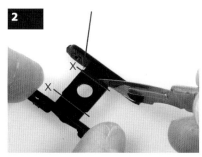

1. The Hornby 'Seacow' has the opposite problem for the finescale modeller compared to the Bachmann product. There is insufficient room between the sideframes to comfortably fit EM or P4 wheels. Furthermore, the sideframes are too

close together and the bearing holes too shallow to accept wheel sets with the standard 26mm axle. Those modellers who wish to use finescale OO gauge wheels must choose wheel sets with 25.5mm axles or modify the bogies as described

below to make room.
2. The centre part of each bogie moulding is removed by scoring along the indicated lines and snapping the sideframes off.
3. Drill out the axle boxes to accept pinpoint

4. Insert a type of bearing called a 'waisted' bearing. These take up less room than a normal top hat bearing.
5. New spacers are fitted to the bogies, placing the sideframes 23 mm apart. A piece of 40 thou

styrene measuring 23mm by 10mm is used for the job and a new hole to accept the pivot screw is drilled in the centre with a 2.5mm diameter drill. The assembly can be modified to accept the Hornby tension lock coupling.

6. The pivot moulding on the model is also changed to accept the modified bogies as shown by the red arrow. Note how a No.5 Kadee coupling has been fitted to the wagon frame.

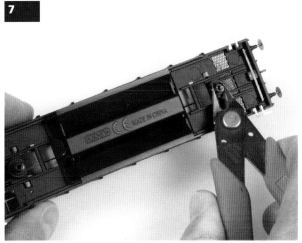

7. Most of the pivot relating to the original bogie is cut away, leaving the large part of the pivot.
8. The remains of the pivot are cleaned up to the level of the large boss,

but do not remove any of the large boss beyond the work required to obtain a flat surface for the bogie to sit on. Once happy, fit the modified bogies using the original screws.

Detailing the 'Seacows'

Some of the bogie ballast hopper wagon fleet is equipped with generators and lighting for engineering work during the night. Those wagons equipped with generators are named 'Stingray' (an additional side screen and mesh guard shields the generator bay at the end of the wagon without braking equipment) and these are fitted with simple jumper cables to connect to those 'Seacows' and 'Sealions' fitted with lighting. It is possible to model this variation with scraps of styrene, some 0.45mm brass wire to represent lighting conduit and careful

'Sealion' and 'Stingray'

1. The side screen is fettled from a small piece of 20thou styrene measuring 13mm high by 9.5mm wide, with the corner nipped off. An opening 4mm high by 3mm wide is cut into the middle of the styrene for the ventilation hole.
2. A quick check to see that it fits the Bachmann model. It took three attempts to obtain a satisfactory result. Don't always go with the first result if you are not entirely happy with it.
3. A piece of etched mesh is fitted to the ventilation hole.

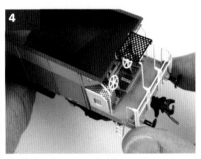

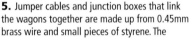

4. The bay is protected with a mesh guard which is made from an off-cut of tank wagon walkway left over from the last chapter! It goes to show that left-over pieces of detailing and other items should never be discarded.
5. Jumper cables and junction boxes that link the wagons together are made up from 0.45mm brass wire and small pieces of styrene. The styrene used for the junction boxes was cut from Evergreen styrene strip No.146 (40 x 125 thou) to a length of 2.5mm. This is a tricky little job to complete and the use of slightly oversize strip makes it a tad easier to drill a 0.45mm hole through it to accept the wire. Note the addition of a large junction box on the opposite side of the platform from the generator bay which measures 9mm tall and 8mm wide, composed of two layers of 40 though styrene.
6. The completed job on the 'Stingray' before weathering. The narrow red line which enhances the livery denotes this vehicle's role as a generator wagon. The junction box is painted grey, as is the generator bay cover and guard. They are occasionally painted orange on some wagons.

7. Transfers to renumber and rename the wagon were taken from a variety of different sheets for engineers' wagons.

8. A bright and clean 'Stingray' poses on the author's portable layout. It's really too clean and weathering will do much to tone down the bright livery.

detail painting. This is how I modified two Bachmann 'Seacows' using reference photographs to check the details. Pictures of a 'Stingray' and modified 'Seacows' are provided at the end of the chapter.

Upgrading the Heljan 'Dogfish'

The green version of Heljan's 'Dogfish' forms the basis of this conversion to P4 gauge together with a description of some simple work to refine the model. Romford 2mm diameter flangeless bearings, a set of three-hole disc wheels and some simple tools are required to complete the re-gauging to P4.

The fitting of new wheels required a little thought because the brake shoes are aligned to the original HO gauge wheels which means that they would be incorrectly positioned for P4. Also, a test fit with the new wheels splayed the axle guards out from the frames, indicating that the axle bearing holes were not deep enough, even though sufficient room was present for the new wheels sets. To correct this, each bearing hole was drilled out by 1mm and a flangeless bearing popped in. Initial tests indicated that each bearing would have to be reduced in length by about half before fitting to the axle box. Once the new wheels were fitted, each brake shoe had to be trimmed and repositioned so not to foul the wheels. Free running of the model took some time to achieve and required careful paring of plastic from the brake shoe mouldings.

The following sequence of pictures shows how the model was refined and re-wheeled.

Simple weathering

The objective of this project is to prepare ballast wagons for service in about an hour of modelling time by applying a light to moderate layer of grime and rust, particularly to the inside of the hopper. It's not intended to show the creation of a seriously battered vehicle! With model finishes being so good, I retain original paint finishes whenever I can, especially

1. Much can be done to upgrade this unassuming model. The wheels can be replaced with three-hole disc wheels (A), the bracket used to strengthen the footsteps can be removed (B) and the chunky handrails enhanced with brass wire (C and D). If so inclined, this pristine model is begging for a weathering job!(E).

2. Remove the strengthening bracket that links the footsteps with the brake shoe. An alternative method of strengthening the footsteps is by drilling a hole through the floor of the model immediately behind each step and inserting a short length of brass wire.

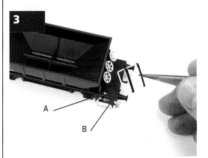

3. The handrails are removed, leaving a spigot at (A) and a hole at (B) which can be used to fit new handrails made up from brass wire.
4. Converting the model to P4 gauge is the most difficult part of the project. New wheels come in the form of Ultrascale three-hole disc wheel sets (A).

The original wheels removed from the model can be thrown away (B) because after modifying the underframe to accept 26mm axles, the original ones will no longer fit. A Brook-Smith back-to-back gauge is used to check that the replacement wheels are in gauge (C).

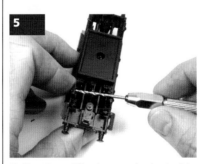

5. Use a 2mm drill to increase the depth of the axle holes by 1.5mm, taking care not to drill through the front of the axlebox cover.

6. Romford plain bearings are filed down to half their original length before fitting to the model.

when it is a good match to the prototype. Some minor changes can be made such as renumbering and re-lettering using transfer sheets. Weathering is applied to give the model a degree of customisation so it appears as a cohesive part of a layout rather than standing out as the

'new' model. Weathering is a personal thing; emphasis can be on either light weathering to tone down the factory paint finish and to give the model character in a short modelling session. Alternatively, you could go for the 'rust bucket' and some 'Seacow' and 'Sealion' ballast hoppers certainly fit this category!

Reference photographs will show how a wagon rusts and weathers in use and I hope the pictures at the end of the chapter will provide an idea of how far you can go if you really wish!

Useful materials and tools:

- **Paint stirrers:** Lolly sticks make excellent paint stirrers and are ideal for digging the gunge out of the bottom of paint jars, the very stuff that is ideal for certain weathering techniques.
- **Paintbrushes:** An older, worn paintbrush is ideal for dry brushing. Better quality ones should be reserved for the application of washes, streaks and block colours.
- **Lint free rag:** Useful for wiping excess paint from a model following the application of a colour wash. Traces of the paint will stick in and around detail and corners giving a subtle, weathered appearance.
- **Plastic container lids:** Save the lids from plastic food containers such as margarine tubs and 'Pringles' tubes and use them as mixing trays.
- **Suitable paint colours:** Light and dark rust from Railmatch; yellows for light rust effects when mixed with dark rust paints together with stone colours for ballast dust and track colour.
- **Thinners:** Paints can be 'bled' onto surfaces by careful use of paint thinner and solvents.
- **Airbrush:** A final dusting of paint is applied with an airbrush.
- **Make-up sponges:** for sponge stippling effects.

When you have prepared your materials and a safe working area with good ventilation, it is time to start work.

Structural modifications and detailing work are completed first, as described earlier in the chapter. Weathering commences with attention to the interior of the hopper and finishes with airbrush dusting. The adjacent step-by-step photographs show how you can weather your ballast hoppers. Remember not to overdo it and that the demonstrated weathering is a many-stage process - colour washes for general grime and dry brushing (or sponging) of rust colours followed by a dusting of brake dust and ballast dust colour with the airbrush to blend it all together. Here's a couple of examples of light to moderate weathering projects using a Heljan 'Dogfish' as an example. Further examples of weathering techniques which can be applied to ballast hoppers are described in the last chapter including the creation of rust buckets.

Weathering the Heljan 'Dogfish' ballast wagon

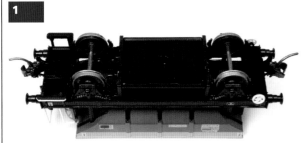

1. The model has been fitted with scale wheels and Kadee couplings. Despite comments to the contrary from some quarters, it is possible to convert the model to EM and P4 gauge.

2. Small modifications made to the model before weathering include removal of the footstep brackets (A) and drilling out axle boxes to accept pin-point bearings (B).

3. Weathering is a lot of fun and the chance to use different colours to apply a worn and used appearance on an otherwise pristine model cannot be resisted! The basic ingredients for a

weathering job are shown, including enamel and acrylic paints.
4. Dig deep into the paint jar for the thick stuff that normally lurks in the bottom following storage.

This is ideal for a variety of weathering techniques.
5. Creating a palette of different colours for rust: Railmatch light rust, red and yellow can be mixed to create different colours of rust.

6. The abrasive action of discharging ballast leaves the hopper prone to rusting. Apply a wash of dark rust to the interior of the hopper. Brush marks should follow the natural path of discharge, i.e. downwards. A tiny quantity of turps or other paint solvent can be used to

bleed the paint over the surface.
7. To represent a wagon recently emptied and left unused for a short period, a second light rust colour mixed from yellow and red is sparingly brushed in a downward pattern.
8. Exterior weathering is a mixture of ballast

dust and track dirt. Dust from discharged ballast mixes with rain water and damp, collecting in the corners of ribs and plating. Vallejo sand yellow acrylic paint is washed over the sides of the model.

9. Use the hem of your T-shirt or better still, a lint free rag to wipe off excess paint to leave traces in the corners of ribs and plating.
10. Unpainted metal details on the 'Dogfish'

model such as ballast discharge gear is touched in with dark grey paint to remove the shine.
11. So far, so good! Things are looking a little less pristine and the model gives the

impression of use and abuse. However, the weathering is still garish and a final process is used to tone it down.

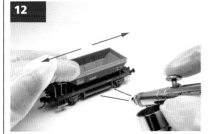

12. Apply a dusting of track colour to the underframe and sides of the hopper. Roll the model from side to side with your finger to avoid paint shadows on the wheels.

13. With your airbrush positioned a reasonable distance from the model, lightly dust stone coloured paint into the hopper and across the end platforms. This tones down the bright rust colours without obliterating them.

14. Weathering is completed by brushing sparing amounts of dark grey around brake shoes and axle boxes to represent grease and oil staining. Note how rusting effects have been applied to the discharge chute too.

15. The finished product. The two-part process of weathering gives the model a completely different appearance. Using an airbrush to dust a final coat of dirt over the model tones any garish colours down a little and brings out moulded detail.

Weathering can bring a model to life, highlighting moulded detail and enhancing the appearance of the model.

The green 'Dogfish' ballast wagon is shown heavily weathered in this picture; with dark rust and grime colours used to give the appearance of a hard worked and unloved wagon. Particular attention is paid to the interior of the hopper where ballast abrades the steel, causing rusting and ballast dust coats everything! Modellers should note that the use of paint solvents will attack the printed lettering, so some care is needed.

YGB No. DB980091 was photographed at Didcot on March 4, 2004. It was observed in weathered and faded 'Dutch' yellow/grey livery. This wagon was constructed at Shildon in 1981.

LEFT: This picture taken at the virtual quarry located in Hinksey Yard Oxford shows how the ballast sits in a fully loaded 'Seacow'. Note the light fitting attached to the platform canopy.

BELOW: 'Sealions' still exist in 2008: this one was photographed at Doncaster in March 2008, still painted in 'Loadhaul' orange and black. It is numbered DB982911 and sports extended canopies too.

A 'Seacow' fitted with lighting equipment and the jumper cables on the platform rails. Note the now faded yellow grey livery with narrow grey line through the yellow to identify it as a lighted wagon but with no generator bay. This wagon is numbered DB992496. The electrical junction box for the lighting equipment is located on the opposite platform, out of sight on the opposite side.

A good example of a 'Stingray' observed from the electrical equipment end. The junction and switch box is nearest the camera, the generator bay on the opposite side of the platform. Note the yellow grey 'Dutch' livery and the red line through the yellow band. This wagon is one of the newer 1981 constructed 'Seacows' as represented by the Hornby model.

ABOVE: One for the EWS fans; YGA No. 980203 has been converted to air brake-only status by removal of the through vacuum brake pipe and features an extended canopy. The basic wagon is represented by the Hornby model. It may be possible to swap canopies around between the Bachmann and Hornby models to achieve the desired combinations!

LEFT: YGB No. 980063 was photographed in rust bucket condition. This wagon is typical of the condition of many 'Seacows' and 'Sealions' in 2008. Features include:
A: Electrification warning signs.
B: A single safety canopy on each end platform.
C: Air brake distributor unit.
D: The vacuum pipe (connected to the through pipe) is missing.
E: Instanter coupling (shackle).
F: Air brake pipe.

Yellow/grey Engineers' livery is applied to 'Dogfish' No.DB983157 which appears to be in reasonable condition. Note the addition of a blue 'Mainline' logo. This wagon was constructed in 1957 by Charles Roberts to Diagram 1/587 as part of Lot 2939. It was photographed at Warrington Arpley in April 1996.

Warrington Arpley is the location of this view of 'Dogfish' No.DB993097 constructed in 1957 by Charles Roberts to Diagram 1/587 as part of Lot 2821. It was photographed in September 1992.

How to weather the interior of a 'Dogfish'. This photograph of an unidentified wagon provides some insight into the shading and colour of stone dust and rust on the inside of the hopper body. Photographed at Tyne Yard on July 20,1995.

Regular visitors to Tyne Yard will know that a useful road bridge spans the north end offering an excellent vantage point for wagon spotting. 'Dogfish' No.DB993186 was caught by the camera during a shunting move at that location on July 20, 1995. This view could inspire a heavy weathering and distressing project on the Heljan model. DB993186 was built by Metro-Cammell Co. Ltd. in 1956 as part of Lot 2822.

When photographed at Westbury in January 1999 'Dogfish' No.DB993256 was stored in a sorry condition at the back of the Down Yard. Constructed in 1957 to Diagram 1/587 by Metro-Cammell Co. Ltd. as part of Lot 2822, it is clear from this photograph that the wagon is at the end of its useful life. Note the Transrail logo applied to a black painted patch on an otherwise rusty wagon.

There are many different air braked mineral wagons used on aggregate, spoil and ballast duties which have been built on redundant underframes. They could keep a modeller busy for many months. That would be without any kit-building work too!

By far the widest variety of wagons in the current scene, as far as ready-to-run models are concerned, is the fleet of air-braked mineral wagons, constructed on a variety of redundant underframes. It's a potentially huge subject! Although the primary use for them is for spoil and ballast duties, I have classified these as 'minerals', because many no longer carry departmental wagon codes or prefixes on the numbers. EWS classifies many of its former POA-based ZKA spoil wagons as MKA, the letter M traditionally used in TOPS codes to identify a mineral wagon. They have seen use as scrap metal carriers and for coal traffic, together with aggregates and ballast duties. The Railtrack/

Network Rail CAIB-registered PNA ballast and spoil wagons are classified as private owner with the letter P in the TOPS code. The PNA fleet could take up a whole chapter on its own anyway, there being so many different wagons within the fleet.

Rebuild, repair and make-do was the order of the day with this particular group of wagons as they are all, without exception, rebuilt and re-bodied wagons on redundant but otherwise perfectly serviceable underframes, recovered from revenue vehicles, mostly domestic coal hoppers and tank wagons. Some have experienced several stages of rebuilding and modification as the wagons are switched from one type of traffic to another. This has presented mainstream

manufacturers the perfect opportunity to make the most of a single underframe moulding to expand their catalogues with various re-bodied models representing this group of modern air braked spoil, ballast and mineral wagons. The Bachmann TTA tank wagon underframe has seen much use, with two types of PNA, several wagons based on the Tiger Rail POA (including the BR converted ZKA 'Limpet' and EWS MKA) and the EWS MTA being offered.

For the modeller who wishes to introduce some variety to their collection, there is so much that can be done with this collection of ready-to-run models. This chapter looks at improving the detail on the Bachmann wagons based on the TTA chassis and how to model a later bodied EWS MHA. The Bachmann PNA has much potential and the use of a different underframe to introduce variation in the fleet is demonstrated too. With there being so many variations and liveries, I can only offer a flavour of the modelling potential in the following pages. Before looking at those modelling opportunities, here is a brief summary of the different types:

Former HBA/HEA domestic coal hopper wagons

The boundary between one type of wagon and another can be blurred when a common underframe is used. HEAs are domestic coal hoppers and 1,998 were built between 1976 and 1979, to replace ageing mineral wagons as HBA with manual door control equipment. HAA type door control equipment was seen as too expensive to install at domestic coal depots at the time. The HEA code was applied to distinguish those wagons fitted with upgraded Bruninghaus suspension which was eventually applied to all of them. As domestic coal traffic dwindled, many HEA wagons were stored and eventually re-bodied to create a modern box mineral wagon, the MEA. Several versions of this wagon were constructed in the early 1990s, following some experimentation with five redundant HAA wagon underframes.

The first batch were built for coal traffic and were fitted with one end ladder and a lamp iron on the box body. They were numbered 391000-082 and painted in 'Railfreight' sector colours complete with a small coal sector logo. Most, if not all, saw use in South Wales, together with the five experimental wagons built on HAA underframes.

The second batch were built for 'Mainline' freight and turned out in blue with white applied to the top rib. No end ladders were fitted to this batch, which were used on industrial coal and aggregate traffic. They were numbered M391101-160.

The next batch were constructed for 'Loadhaul' to the same specification as the 'Mainline' freight examples, being painted black with a white top rib. They were numbered 391201-240 and used on industrial coal traffic.

EWS authorised further MEAs, the wagons being fitted with two ladders, one on each end. Numbered 391241-630, they were used on a variety of traffic flows including aggregates and industrial coal together with ballast and spoil traffic. It is the latter two traffics which saw the introduction of the MFA, a cut down version of the MEA, designed to avoid overloading with spoil, a particularly dense material, which can easily load a wagon to capacity without filling the body!

MFA wagons are cut down MEA box mineral wagons and many of the conversions were simply patch painted after the work was complete. Some were cut from the top down, recognised by new paint applied along the top half of the wagon. Others were shortened in height from the bottom of the body and new paint was applied accordingly. MFAs retained their original MEA numbers. HEAs, MEAs and MFAs remain in traffic as of 2008, in a variety of liveries and various stages of rusting!

In one form of mineral wagons, some HEAs were utilised on scrap traffic, the hopper doors being sealed and ballast placed inside the wagon to prevent

The Bachmann MEA, a re-use of the HEA underframe. This is the older version with heavily moulded brake gear on a chunky underframe, which has subsequently been re-tooled by Bachmann.

Bachmann offers the cut-down MEA too, in various liveries. The wagon in the background is an older model with the original underframe which has been weathered. The body shows patch painting to represent where the body was cut down from an MEA. The foreground model is straight from the box and has the later retooled underframe, which has much fine detail.

LEFT: Unfortunately, the NEM coupling pockets do not meet the NEM standards set down by MOROP. Stepped tension lock couplings are fitted to compensate, but Kadee and other NEM coupling users will be at a disadvantage! These models were in the process of being prepared for service on my layout, being fitted with EM gauge wheels with etched brake discs.

BELOW: This is an example of the 'Loadhaul' black model with added EWS logo. Many of the former freight company liveries still exist on these wagons, with an EWS logo.

Hornby has reused its HAA underframe to offer a model of the EWS MHA spoil and ballast wagon. After an initial hiccup with the body, the Hornby MHA is now regarded as a pretty good representation of the full-size wagon, although only the first type of MHA is represented, in the number range 394001-400. The model can be further enhanced by replacing the inaccurate buffers, removing the lamp iron from the headstocks and adding details such as brake hoses. Weathering really brings these models to life.

The Bachmann MTA is a further use of the TTA underframe and offers another choice for EWS modellers to expand their mineral wagon collections.

magnetic grabs from lifting them from the rails during unloading. These wagons retained their HEA numbers but were recoded HSA. They can be simply modelled using an HEA model, suitably battered, of course!

To complete the story, noteworthy conversions using the HEA underframe include the three scrap wagon prototypes, the SJAs (360040, 360761 and 361486) which were painted 'Railfreight' red and were, in effect, fore-runners of the MEAs. Also, some HEAs were used as RNA runner wagons, which are ballasted HEA underframes without the hopper. They were used with nuclear flask wagons and can be modelled using a cast metal detailing insert from Genesis Kits. Finally, some HEAs were fitted with covers and coded CEA, randomly chosen from the fleet and retaining their original HEA numbers.

MHA 'Coalfish'

The first use of HAA MGR coal hopper wagon underframes to create box mineral wagons was the conversion of five HAAs to mineral wagons numbered 392000-004 which saw use in South Wales. The bodies were cut down as part of the MFA conversion programme and renumbered 394406-410, coded MHA, not being fully repainted in the process. EWS authorised more MHAs, the wagons being re-bodied

MGR wagons with low side bodies from new. As construction progressed, the design was simplified, with a box sporting fewer ribs and no ladder detail.

EWS MTA wagons

MTA wagons are low-side spoil and ballast wagons, built on the underframes of SUKO-registered 'Shell' TTA tank wagons, with the odd 'Esso' TTA thrown in. There is a patchy record as to which TTA became which MTA. They are numbered 395001-241, without a prefix and with some gaps in the sequence. The body is a simple rib reinforced box, with the sides and ends of equal height unlike the similar 'Doorand' type. It was an obvious choice for Bachmann's one-fits-all TTA chassis.

POA, ZKA and MKA mineral wagon

The ZKA is a modified POA and PNA box mineral wagon once used for aggregate and lime traffic, which were constructed in 1987 and 1988 on the recovered underframes from TTA tank wagons by C C Crump at Connah's Quay, amongst others. These wagons were subsequently acquired by the BR 'Intercity' sector for use as ballast and spoil wagons, after they had been made redundant by the introduction of large capacity bogie box wagons for aggregate traffic. There is some debate regarding the timing and the extent of modifications undertaken by 'Intercity' and many of them were put into use with minimal attention, including retention of their original private owner liveries, which can still be seen under the rust on some examples today. The wagons were renumbered in the DC390150-331 number sequence and TOPS coded ZKA. It is worth noting that MKAs were numbered as 393000-393035, although there are records of MKA coded wagons in the DC390xxx sequence, re-coded from the ZKA code and with side-slots which can cause some confusion.

ZKA wagons were modified by the cutting of side-slots in the two central panels of each side, to prevent the

The plain grey example of Bachmann's new ZKA wagon model is numbered DC390168 and marked with contemporary electrification warning flashes. It should be noted that the real 390168 had been re-coded as an MKA at the time of writing.

Bachmann researched the departmental 'Dutch' yellow and grey livery particularly well, including the application of the claret Intercity logo. One notable feature of the POA/MKA/ZKA is that the sides and ends of the body moulding are quite thick, being 2mm in width across the top rib. The interior has been painted in a pleasing dark rust colour which is ideal base for the application of further weathering effects.

The use of one TTA underframe as a 'one size fits all' is not ideal for all MKA and ZKA wagons, and Bachmann should consider tooling additional components to enable different variations in the TTA underframe to be modelled to suit individual wagons. The suspension springs are not correct for MTA, PNA and POA wagons either. This detail can be changed by using simple detailing parts as seen later in the chapter.

The seven-rib PNA from Bachmann which utilises its standard TTA underframe. There is a typo in the 'Railtrack' branding. It should read 'Railway', not 'Railways'. It is easily corrected by gently scraping the offending letter away with a scalpel blade. Later releases by Bachmann have seen this typo corrected.

wagon from being overloaded with spoil. Not all of the fleet were initially treated and a number of these were used in revenue freight traffic, particularly for the haulage of coal with 'Loadhaul' and scrap metal. Many were re-coded MKA, identifying them for use in revenue traffic as mineral wagons and they became the last to be modified for spoil and ballast traffic by the addition of bodyside slots. These could be identified by the patch painting, where additional ribs have been fitted as part of the cutting of slots in the sides.

Many ZKA wagons retained their original POA private owner liveries, with some partial painting to represent their new roles and in some cases some were painted in the pre-privatisation liveries such as 'Mainline' blue and 'Loadhaul' orange and black. It is possible to see, even today, traces of 'ARC' branding with partial application of 'Dutch' yellow and

grey engineers' livery and 'Loadhaul' orange and black, with patch painting to indicate that bodyside slots had been cut into the wagon after painting in that livery. The modeller should be alert to variations in the fleet, as all is not what it may seem and the use of reference photographs is critically important to identify your chosen prototype and to discover if it was modified for spoil traffic within your chosen time period.

Railtrack PNA ballast and spoil wagons

Anyone who has taken the time to research Railtrack/CAIB ballast and spoil wagons will have discovered that, within the fleet of 250 vehicles, there is variation in both underframes and the bodies themselves. It can be a potential modelling minefield! The reason for this is simple; the wagons were constructed using underframes recovered from

redundant wagons including 45 and 46 tonne TTA tank wagons, former 'Tunnel Cement' and 'Castle Cement' bulk powder tanks, TUA tank wagons and other odds and ends that happened to be lying around.

Some vehicles are constructed on underframes recovered from wagons fitted with BSC Axle Motion suspension units ('Tunnel Cement' PCAs No. TC9490-93 and 'Castle Cement' PCAs from the RBL10400-443 series), and tank wagons coded TUA from the 70xxx sequence, which were fitted with Gloucester suspension. You can trace the number sequence using the basic TTA underframe from CAIB 3600 to CAIB 3749, with both body formats produced by Bachmann. To model CAIB 3750-3849, you enter the realm of conversion and scratch-building of the various underframes, together with looking at various changes to the wagon body.

What's available
1. Bachmann MEA and MFA
Bachmann offer both the MEA and the cut down MFA in a variety of liveries and with a relatively new chassis, which has refined detail, including fine brake levers and brake gear. The NEM coupling pocket is set too high when compared to the MOROP standards and has to be corrected if Kadee couplers or Continental close coupling systems are to be used.

The PNA is another use of the general TTA underframe produced by Bachmann and is a very useful model indeed, the five-rib body being appropriate for a number of simple conversions. Bachmann has equipped its PNA models with NEM coupling sockets and three-hole disc wheels. The coupling pocket is not to the NEM specification for height from the rail for the use of Kadee couplings designed to fit NEM pockets.

2. Hornby MHA

This model represents the first type of EWS MHA using the HAA underframe. The buffers are incorrect for MHAs and the character of the model is changed by simply fitting the correct pattern of Oleo buffer. NEM coupling pockets are correctly fitted, although set well back behind the headstocks. No.20 Kadee couplers are an ideal choice for this wagon.

3. Bachmann MTA

The MTA is a further use of the Bachmann TTA chassis; a body with fine detail and good printed livery elements on the one-size-fits-all chassis. It has real potential for detailing, including replacement of the inaccurate suspension springs. The TTA underframe used on this wagon and the following models has NEM coupling pockets which are not to the specification laid down in the MOROP NEM standards. The NEM pocket is mounted too high for use with NEM standard Kadee couplings and modifying the chassis to bring it into line with this standard could prove to be less than straightforward for many modellers.

4. Bachmann POA, ZKA and MKA

The underframe used on this group of models has the same early suspension spring detail instead of parabolic (Bruninghaus) springs which are exclusively used on this type of wagon.

It is possible to make a simple change to the Bachmann TTA underframe used under its MTA, POA, MKA and PNA models to update the suspension detail. Firstly, remove the brake levers so that they are not damaged during the process.

No attempt has been made to produce further components to introduce the different variations in underframe detail that can be found, despite the fact that the underframe is modular to allow changes in detail.

Turning my attention to the new body tooling, it appears to me that the bodyside and the bodyside ribs are too thick and chunky when compared to the prototype. The bodyshell side is 2mm across the width of the top rib which is a massive 6" to scale. Bachmann has carefully researched the liveries for these wagons as far as I can tell. The 'Dutch' yellow/grey engineers' version is numbered DC390153 and I was successful in finding photographs

of that particular wagon, confirming that that was the correct livery. The other model was the plain grey version which is numbered DC390168. That too is correctly painted and the markings are also pretty close. Livery application in the case of both models was sharp and accurate with good colour density.

6. Bachmann PNA

Bachmann have taken advantage of its TTA underframe, originally tooled for its tank wagon models, to produce the PNA, which includes two types; a five-rib version and seven-rib version suitable for that type of underframe, keeping tooling cost of the minimum

Take a sharp modelling knife and cut through the moulded springs on either side of the axle guards. Do not remove the spring hangers.

Pare the moulded spring from the surface of the axle guards so it is completely flat and ready to accept moulded spring detail.

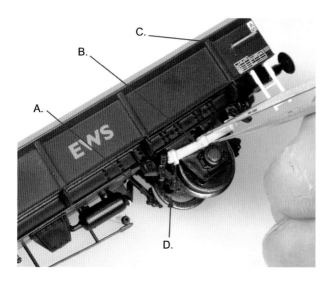

C.

B.

A.

EWS

D.

LEFT: New parabolic 'Bruninghaus' spring detail is added with a drop of glue (B). Whilst looking at this picture, it is worth noting that the underframe could be further detailed by adding brake yokes to the clasp brakes (A). Also, the bright metal handrails are treated with primer so that they can be painted white (C). The three hole disc wheels fitted by Bachmann are technically correct for this type of wagon (D).

BELOW: This simple improvement can be made to all of the wagons featured in this chapter that are based on the TTA underframe (as seen in this picture).

and resulting in a very attractive price for each model.

As has been noted before, the basic tank wagon underframe produced by Bachmann has older suspension detail which is not appropriate for the PNA (or modern versions of the TTA). The brake detail on the underframe is generalised to save on tooling costs and consequently it will not exactly match many of the PNAs in traffic today, especially the brake hangers and brake levers. Nonetheless, it forms the basis for a detailed model if the suspension springs are replaced and brake equipment is modified to suit a particular prototype. The note regarding the NEM coupling pockets also applies to this model.

Upgrading the Bachmann MFA model

1

2

3

1. One of the problems with the Bachmann MEA and MFA is the incorrectly positioned NEM coupling pocket which is fitted too high, as demonstrated in this picture. Seen to the left of the wagon is a Kadee coupling height gauge.

2. It is possible to correct the height of the NEM coupling pocket. Release the screws at (A) to remove the ballast weight and the coupling pockets (B). Part of the coupling pocket moulding is a bush which secures the weight in

place. Take care not to damage the brake distributor moulding at (C).
3. This collection of parts is what you should end up with when dismantling the underframe.

4

5

6

4. Firstly, remove the moulded spigots from the underframe at each end of the wagon as shown by the red arrow.
5. As mentioned earlier, the NEM pocket

moulding includes a plastic bush which secures the ballast weight in place. Cut the bush off the mouldings and place to one side for reuse.
6. The modified NEM coupling pocket moulding is

glued to the wagon floor behind the headstocks as indicated by the red arrow. Before gluing it in place, a pad made of styrene is fitted to adjust the height of the pocket relative to the wagon floor.

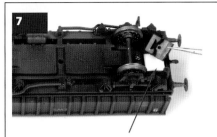

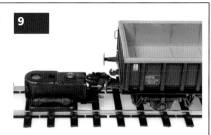

7. This picture shows the pad of 30thou styrene glued in place. Normally, it is a good idea to use black styrene. White has been used here so that it is visible in the photograph.

8. The finished job with NEM pockets glued to the styrene pads and correctly fitted to the right operating height to allow No.18 Kadee couplings to be used. The underframe has been screwed back together using the plastic bushes

to secure everything in place as it was before.
9. Don't forget to use the appropriate gauge to check the height of your couplings before putting the model into use.

10. A picture of the real thing showing how battered these wagons become after years of abuse. It is in original Railfreight livery as applied to this wagon when it was converted from an HEA to MEA. Conversion to an MFA simply involved the removal of half the body height. Some were modified from floor level (apparently) and some from the top as in the

case of 391058. You can identify this by the patch painting! The coal sector logo was lost many years ago, although some MFAs still sport them under the grime.
11. This model has been painted with patching to replicate the same effect on the full-size wagons.

Modelling a different PNA to the Bachmann model

In the introduction to this chapter, it was mentioned that the Railtrack CAIB PNA wagons have many variations, as a result of the recovered tank wagon underframes used to build these wagons. It is worthwhile looking at reference photographs, to see what can be created with a Bachmann PNA body and an underframe from a different model. CAIB 3750-94 is one such subject for a simple conversion, based on the former TC9490-3 and RBL 104xx PCAs, where a Bachmann body can be mated with a Bachmann POA scrap steel carrier, with some detail changes and minor scratch building. Investigation into using the Hornby PCA Vee-tank

wagon chassis shows that it is too short to be of any real value in modelling PNAs with Gloucester suspension.

In reality, the bodies of PNAs varied slightly in length to suit the length of the underframe used and as a result, such conversions may not be completely accurate to the millimetre if using the Bachmann body – finescale modellers could resort to a mixture of scratch-building and the use of underframes from other models. For example, the CAIB 3829-49 series, based on former TUAs with Gloucester suspension, is 103.5mm over headstocks and has a different body rib arrangement too. CAIB 3817-28 is documented as being 106mm over headstocks, with a body fitted with seven evenly spaced ribs. Both these wagons

would be better scratch-built rather than attempting to utilise the Bachmann body.

Nonetheless, creating variation in one's wagon collection is as important as finescale accuracy, and wagons numbered CAIB 3750-94 used recovered PCA underframes which were 28´-8˝over buffers. The length over headstocks is 101mm, which suits the Bachmann wagon body – the closest match possible to model, using the underframe from the Bachmann POA/SSA, which has to be shortened slightly to suit.

Other details were added to make the resulting model as close to the prototype as possible. The following sequence of pictures shows how this type of wagon was created, whilst retaining as much of the original body livery as possible.

1. PNA No. CAIB 3777 is a good example of a conversion that can use the five-rib body and the Bachmann POA scrap steel carrier underframe. CAIB 3777 has some other interesting features. Originally built on the recovered underframe from a RBL 104xx 'Castle Cement' PCA, it has BSC Pedestal

suspension, clasp brakes and short brake levers. Length over buffers is 28' 8"(114.5mm). In other words, an interesting project.
2. The project combines the body of the Bachmann PNA and underframe from the scrap wagon seen in the rear of this picture.

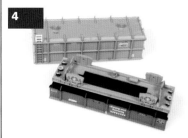

4. The new underframe is a close fit, only being a couple of millimetres over-length to fit the body.

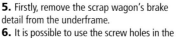

5. Firstly, remove the scrap wagon's brake detail from the underframe.
6. It is possible to use the screw holes in the

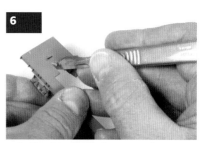

underside of the PNA body to secure the new underframe. Modify the underframe by extending the slots to clear the screw hole spigots.

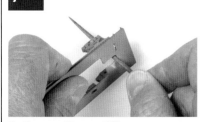

7. Clean up with a round file.
8. Test fit the underframe to the body as you go along as seen in this picture. The screw spigots can be seen at (A), whilst a moulded rib

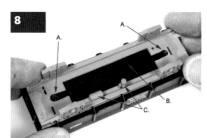

located at (B) is found to prevent body and underframe from coming together neatly. Remove and save the brake equipment fitted to the underframe at (C).

9. A sharp modelling knife makes short work of paring the moulded rib from the underside of the body.

10. This picture shows the underframe screwed in place. Note that the underframe has been shortened so that new headstocks consisting of

40thou styrene can be glued between the end of the underframe and the body.
11. Clasp brake mouldings are fitted next, using

the wheels as a guide to placing them correctly.
12. The headstocks and buffers follow up on the brake gear.

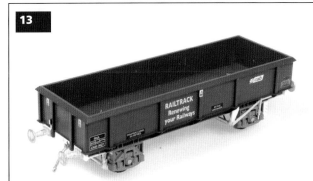

13

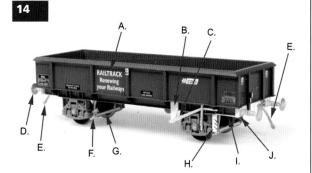

14

A. B. C. E. D. E. F. G. H. I. J.

13. The finished result with the new detail visible in unpainted plastic, brass and cast metal.

14. A. As much of the original livery is saved as possible to save time and money in avoiding a repaint of the body. Paint over the letter S on the word 'Railways'.
B. New brake lever bracket made from 20thou styrene.
C. Short brake lever taken from a detailing etch by Mainly Trains.
D. Small diameter 'Oleo' buffer castings by S Kits.

E. Lost wax brake pipes by Inter-City Models.
F. White metal clasp brake details.
G. Brass brake yokes taken from a detailing etch by Mainly Trains.
H. Brake lever ratchet made from 10thou styrene.
I. Styrene strip was used to modify the solebars to remove a step at the headstocks.
J. New headstocks made of 40thou styrene.

Converting a POA to ZKA

1

2

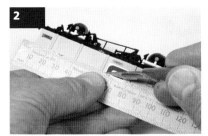

3

1. A model with a great deal of potential for weathering, different liveries and some unusual hybrid liveries as changes in use have occurred is the Bachmann POA. By removing the ladders and cutting overload slots in the sides, it can be

converted to a ZKA whilst retaining as much of the original livery as possible in the same manner as the full size wagons, where it is still possible to see original livery details underneath patch painting and grime.

2. The position of overload slots is marked in with a scalpel blade. The slots should be 6mm deep.
3. Drill a network of holes within the measurements marked with the scalpel blade, taking care not to damage the rib detail.

4

5

4. Cut through the drill holes as shown in this picture and clean up with a file.
5. A new rib composed of 40thou x 60thou styrene strip is added beneath the slots. Ideally, strip measuring 40thou x 70thou would be better but

was unavailable at the time. Patch painting, re-coding and weathering will complete the job. Don't forget to remove the ladders!

There are two versions of the EWS MHA wagon and it is the first version of it that is represented by the Hornby model. No. 394259 is a typical MHA, although it does not carry the name 'Coalfish'. Note that the buffers are a different type to that fitted to the model and the following sequence of photographs shows how this model can be corrected.

Improving and converting the Hornby MHA

1. The Hornby MHA with cast metal 'Oleo' buffers fitted. Whilst these bring an improvement to its appearance, the buffer heads are a tad too large.

2. The detail that should be kept is the buffer housing. The buffer heads can be replaced with turned steel ones. Simply cut the cast ones off

and clean up with a file.
3. Drill out the buffer housings with a 0.7mm diameter drill.

4. Turned metal buffer heads are much finer in appearance than cast ones. Steel buffer heads from C&L Finescale were used on this conversion.
5. The second version of the MHA has a simpler style of body with fewer ribs and no ladder detail. This type of MHA is not represented by the Hornby

model even though it rides on underframes recovered from MGR wagons. Also noteworthy is that the ribs are composed of 'I'-section steel and not 'U'-channel as used on the first type. MHA No. 394980 was photographed at Newport, Gwent in April 2004, in near immaculate condition.

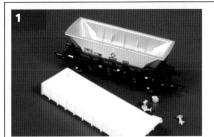

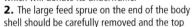

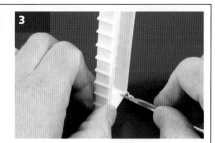

1. The second, later version of the MHA can be modelled using a resin body kit or by scratch-building. A cast resin body kit for this version of the MHA was available from S Kits at the time

of writing. Behind is the Hornby MGR wagon which will donate its underframe.

2. The large feed sprue on the end of the body shell should be carefully removed and the top

rib filed to the correct profile.

3. Some moulding flash was present along the inside of the body which was pared away with a modelling knife.

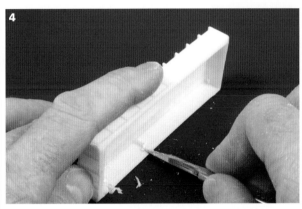

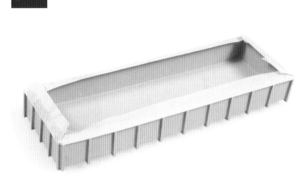

4. This picture shows the cast resin MHA body in the process of being cleaned of moulding flash to prepare it for painting. Care must be taken when handling resin parts to avoid breathing in dust that results from sanding, cutting and filing the work piece.

5. Once all finishing is complete, the body is undercoated with primer and the top rib masked off before painting EWS maroon. Two coats of maroon may be necessary for total coverage.

6 & 7. The completed second version MHA body ready for fitting to a MGR wagon underframe. Locating spigots are present on the underside of the resin body to locate it properly on the underframe. Some trimming of the spigots may be necessary.

Completed models

LEFT: The yellow and grey departmental liveried ZKA is a popular version of the model. Weathering has toned down the otherwise bright livery. Rusting effects are added using quick drying Burnt Sienna oil paint.

RIGHT: Simple detailing and the application of rusting and brake dust weathering has taken the factory finish off this Bachmann ZKA model.

BELOW: Bachmann's PNA model quickly assumes the character of a hard worked wagon with the application of brake dust, ballast dust and rust.

LEFT: Weathering should also be applied to the interior of the model. Paint the interior, if required, in dark rust and then use a light sandy brown colour to create the marks left from various loads of ballast and spoil. These wagons are emptied with mechanical grabs, so not all of the load is removed.

RIGHT: The Bachmann MTA wagon with dirt and some new details.

BELOW: This is the unweathered result of the PNA conversion described earlier in the chapter.

ABOVE: Further character has been added to this MFA by adding rust spots and patches together with rust streaking.

LEFT: Another view of a Bachmann PNA. Kadee couplings have been fitted at the correct operating height. Unfortunately, the NEM coupling pockets were abandoned and No. 5 couplers used instead.

BELOW: This model looks quite different from its pristine appearance from earlier in the chapter.

This is an interesting photograph because it is the actual ZKA represented by the Bachmann model painted in plain grey. However, by the time I took this photograph it had been re-coded MKA and the DC prefix had been painted over. Note that the underframe is of a slightly different format to that represented by the Bachmann model. MKA No. 390168 was photographed at Newport on April 26, 2004.

The third model of the ZKA offered by Bachmann is painted in 'Loadhaul' livery. This photograph is of a typical example with side slots and coded ZKA. ZKA No. DC390268 was photographed at Newport on April 26, 2004.

RIGHT: An interesting detailing project based on the Bachmann POA and using quantities of 40 x 60 thou styrene strip would be MKA No. 390195 which was photographed at Oxford Hinksey Yard in May 2004. This wagon was built on the recovered underframes from TRL51899 by C C Crump in 1987 to become TRL5184. It retains plain grey livery and has overloading slots cut in the sides.

LEFT: A typical example of the breed in severely battered and rusted yellow and grey 'Dutch' livery. This former ZKA No. DC390227 has been re-coded MKA although it (incorrectly) retains the DC prefix. It was photographed at Didcot on November 27, 2003.

BELOW: Former ZKA (MKA) No. DC390193 is a plain grey example in reasonable condition. The data panels are stencilled on black patches. Photographed at Didcot on November 27, 2003.

ABOVE LEFT: Another example of a ZKA retaining scabby remnants of yellow and grey livery is No. 390260, photographed at Oxford Hinksey Yard on May 17, 2004. Few of them have been repainted in recent years and they offer the modeller a chance to experiment with some interesting weathering techniques including rusting and bleaching effects. Note that any access ladders that may have been fitted to this wagon in its days as a POA have been removed.

ABOVE RIGHT: A typical MFA is represented by No. 391017 in 'Railfreight' colours. It appears, from the patch painting, that this wagon was reduced in height from the base of the body. Note the EWS logo and other information panels applied in EWS colours.

RIGHT: MFA No. 391271 was photographed at Westbury and is one of the EWS batch of MEAs to be cut down to MFA size. The original livery is EWS maroon and patch painting suggests that it was cut down from the base of the body.

MHA No. 394410 is one of the small batch of experimental MEA-type box coal wagons built on HAA underframes and subsequently cut down to form the first MHA wagons. In common with the MFAs, the original livery has been retained and patch painting applied to those areas of the body affected by the conversion.

ABOVE: A typical example of an early 'production' MHA including the 'Coalfish' name on the solebar.

LEFT: This picture of an unidentified MFA gives an idea of the weathering effects in the body and how remnants of its last load remain because mechanical grabs can't get it all.

BELOW: Rust and dust is the order of the day for this type of wagon and MHA No. 394215 appears to have plenty of both. The key to adding character to your models is in the weathering and this picture can be used as a guide.

ABOVE LEFT: The second version of 'production' MHA wagons has a simpler body with no footsteps and fewer ribs as seen on No. 394606.

ABOVE RIGHT: Taking a look at the headstocks of an MHA, note that the lamp iron has been removed because one is provided on the body end. This picture also shows the different pattern of rib used on the body.

RIGHT: Underframe detail showing the brake cylinder on a MTA wagon.

BELOW: A typical EWS MTA wagon loaded with fresh ballast.

LEFT: More MTA underframe detail for modellers! This is MTA No. 395155.

BELOW: Another view of MTA No. 395155 showing the scoring of the body which results from the use of mechanical grabs to unload the wagon.

LEFT: This picture shows the end detail of MTA No. 395155.

BELOW: Railtrack PNA wagons are very interesting because of the various underframes used to construct them. PNA No. CAIB 3779 is one of the former Castle Cement PCA wagons and was one of the wagons that inspired the conversion described earlier in the chapter. The Bachmann body is about the correct length to suit this wagon with a length over headstocks of 101mm in 4mm scale.

PNA No. CAIB 3818 has Gloucester suspension and was once TUA Caustic Soda tank wagon No. PR 70151. It is fitted with clasp brakes and a body with seven evenly spaced ribs. The Bachmann PNA body cannot be used because it is too short and with incorrect rib spacing. A scale model would have to be 106mm over headstocks in 4mm scale.

LEFT: An unidentified seven-rib PNA was photographed in a train of mixed PNA wagons during material recovery duties at Sunderland on September 4, 2005.

BELOW: Unlike CAIB 3818, this version with Gloucester suspension is fitted with disc brakes. PNA No.CAIB 3803 was once a TUA tank wagon and carried the number PR70136. Its length over headstocks would be 106mm in 4mm scale and cannot be modelled using the Bachmann body.

PNA No.CAIB 3808 is different again! This wagon is a former TUA Caustic Soda tank No.PR70141. Note the seven evenly spaced body ribs. It is shorter than CAIB 3803 but still too long to suit the Bachmann body, even if the ribs were not spaced differently.

This wagon is a close match to the Bachmann 7-rib version of its PNA model and is constructed on a former TTA underframe. CAIB 3639 was once BRT 57732.

PNA No.CAIB 3635 is also a close match to the Bachmann model.

ABOVE: The five-rib version is represented by CAIB 3653 which was once BRT 57606, a former TTA tank wagon.

RIGHT: Another five-rib version which can be modelled using the Bachmann model is CAIB 3680, formerly BRT 57610.

BELOW: A different version of the seven-rib body is seen on CAIB 3840 which used to be a TUA fuel oil tank, No.BRT 70511. It has Gloucester suspension, disc brakes on two opposing wheels and very little else! Its appearance is very minimalist, with only two disc brake calipers resulting in an uncluttered underframe. When modelling this wagon, be aware that the body will be sized to fit the underframe and not the other way round – the Bachmann body will not fit a model which would be 103.5mm over headstocks in 4mm scale.

MODELLING BRITISH NETWORK INTERMODAL OPERATIONS

Freightliner Class 08, No. 08 575 shuffles wagons at Millbrook in preparation for an early afternoon departure. The two wagons seen behind the locomotive are FEA-B spines, introduced by Freightliner as replacements for the few remaining traditional spine wagons, the FFA and FGA. Various types of FEA wagon have been purchased by other operators too, including GB Railfreight for intermodal operations and others for carrying engineers' modules. At the time of writing, Dapol had released an N gauge model for the FEA-B and an OO gauge model is on its way. The Class 08 can be obtained as an off-the-shelf model from both Hornby and Bachmann.

Using available ready-to-run models and detailing kits to create intermodal operations.

Intermodal is a common term in the freight logistics industry and is regularly used by railway enthusiasts and modellers. But what exactly does it mean? Well, if you do some research of the different definitions for the word 'intermodal' you will encounter many answers. One such definition runs like this: being or involving transportation by more than one form of carrier during a single journey. Well, yes, that just about sums it up. It is useful to know the difference between intermodal and multimodal transport so that we

appreciate the difference when planning railway operations on our layouts.

Here's another definition: intermodal transport is the movement of goods in one and the same loading unit (container) or vehicle (piggyback trailer or swap body) which uses successively several modes of transport, without handling of the goods themselves in changing modes.

For example, the trans-shipment of containers between container ship and pup-trailer rigs at the docks and the onward distribution by rail or road.

There may be a short period when the container is stored in a highly organised, computer controlled storage area. The same container will probably finish its journey by road. This is a distinctly different terminology to multimodal transport, which is the transport of goods by at least two different modes of transport in which the load or goods may be handled during the process. Mail and most steel traffic is a good example of multimodal logistics.

This chapter looks at what can be achieved using available ready-to-run models, containers and detailing kits. From a 4mm scale modellers point of view, only two good-quality intermodal wagons are available of the shelf together with suitable containers, one of which is not commonly seen on the rail network, the Bachmann IFA/FIA intermodal twin wagon and the Dapol FEA-B. You cannot really count the ageing Hornby Freightliner wagon, because, in terms of modern modelling standards, it is little more than a toy. The British outline modeller does not enjoy any products for road vehicles suitable for intermodal operations, nor any terminal equipment specific to intermodal operations in either kit or ready assembled form, except the HO scale DCC intermodal crane from Heljan. Despite the best efforts of a couple of smaller manufacturers that produce some interesting and useful kits, the UK outline intermodal enthusiast has had every right to feel, well, neglected. Only recently hints have emerged regarding further support on the wagon and container front. As it stands at the time of writing, no contemporary off-the-shelf model exists for Freightliner FFA, FGA, FSA, FTA and the low-riding FLA. You cannot buy a FEA-A as used by GB Railfreight together with the other FEAs used on intermodal services and engineers' module use. Also missing are OO gauge IKA Megafret wagons and EWS-operated FAA and FCA container wagons. You have to turn to kits for many of these vehicles or undertake conversions (it is possible to convert the Bachmann intermodal twin into FSA and FTA wagons).

Whilst this chapter is intended to be a useful guide to working with what little is available, I hope that the manufacturers take note of the yawning chasms in trade support and make a real effort to provide some new models to make the modelling of this traffic base more enjoyable. As it is, we can look at the following projects:
• Making the best of the Bachmann

IFA/FIA intermodal twin wagon
• Adapting the Brawa Sffggmrrss wagon.
• Redecorating Bachmann 20´ containers with different liveries.
• Building the C-Rail Intermodal container kits for the 40´. box, 30´. 'Bulktainers' and 20´. tank container to suit the Bachmann intermodal wagon and Dapol FEA-B

Locomotives

There is absolutely no problem with finding suitable traction for intermodal traffic, with Bachmann providing quality models of the Class 57/0 and Class 66/5 in Freightliner livery. You can buy Bachmann Class 66s in EWS, GB Railfreight and DRS colours too. Heljan produced an acceptable Class 47/0 and Bachmann offers a Class 47 model of its own, which will include freight versions suitable for Freightliner working in time. The Hornby Class 56 has a role to play as well, because these locomotives did find use on container trains in the 1980s and today a number of the class operate Fastline's container services to and from Grain. In the late 1980s and early 1990s, some Freightliner workings employed pairs of Class 37/0, painted in RfD livery and model Class 37/0s are available from Bachmann. All of these models are regarded as 'new generation' with quality drives, modern tooling and detail.

Electric traction is commonly rostered for intermodal working and here we have to turn to Hornby for suitable models. All of them are older products that lack the refinement of 'new generation' models and may need some upgrading work to the mechanisms to enable them to haul decent length trains. Hornby offers the Class 86 and 90 in Freightliner colours together with the EWS/RfD Class 92, used extensively on EWS and European intermodal services. Shunting your terminals is no problem with good models of the Class 08 and Class 09 being available from both Bachmann and Hornby.

The Bachmann 'Eurotwin'

Anyone who has attempted to build any type of spine or skeleton wagon from scratch will know how difficult it is to achieve the thinness of section on the frame and also hide enough ballast in the open structure for reliable running. If a large collection of similar wagons is required, scratch-building from brass sheet and section would prove to be a very time consuming job.

With this in mind, the practical difficulties that Bachmann have overcome to offer a quality low platform container wagon in 4mm scale, with all of the individual fittings and within a reasonable development and build cost can be appreciated. The result is a superb quality model at an unbelievable price for a twin-set, and a wise choice, given the almost universal appeal of the IFA 'EuroTwin multifret' wagon to contemporary diesel and electric era (D&E) modellers. This is the first ready-to-run 4mm scale container flat wagon since the release of the now very elderly Hornby Freightliner wagon.

At the time of writing, Bachmann has released several editions of this model, featuring the 45' extended container in different liveries and combinations in each twin-pack, together with others carrying different 20' containers. Bachmann has also released the wagons without containers, so modellers can introduce variety with container kits or to run empty wagons.

225 'EuroTwin' sets or intermodal wagons (code Sfggmmrss) were constructed for Railfreight Distribution and placed in traffic by 1994. Numbered 31 70 49 38 000-224 (now with gaps due to renumbering of some wagons), they were registered in Britain for operation through the Channel Tunnel to European destinations and are TOPS coded IFA. The wagons are permanently coupled in twin-sets and can carry a maximum load of 107.4 tonnes. Two 20' containers or one 30', 40' or 45' container can be carried on each wagon in the twin-set. A loading deck height of 945mm is achieved by the use of small-wheel bogies

Table 1: General loading gauge restrictions

FIA/IFA 'Multifret' FKA/IKA 'Megafret'	Loading (Sfggmrrss) (Sffggmrrss)	Gauge container size
W6	8' 0"	8' 6"
W7	8' 0"	8' 6"
W8	8' 6"	9' 0"
W9	9' 0"	9' 0"
W12	9' 6"	9' 6"

Notes: FIA/IFA loading deck 945mm from rail
IKA loading deck 825mm from rail

Table 2: IFA wagon dimensions

Dimension	Prototype	Model (mm)	+/- (mm)
Length of twin over buffers	36.52m	495	+15 [1]
Width of deck	2.6m	34	0
Length of individual wagons	18.26m	240	0
Deck height from rail	0.945m	12.4	0
Bogie wheelbase	2m	26	0
Container length	13.7m/45'	178	-2
Container height	2.6m/8' 6"	34	0
Container width	2.5m	33	0

[1] Difference is taken by inner coupling bar to ensure operation on tight radius curves and not actually a dimensional error in either.

designated Y33, and a raised end platform with conventional buffers and draw gear. The wagon was rated for 75mph operation on Railtrack, until trials earlier in 2002 demonstrated safe operation at 90mph. Subsequently, selected wagons have been renumbered from the original series into three new sequences, probably to reflect those allocated to freight aggregation companies such as Unilog. These are 33 70 49 38 300-339, 33 70 49 38 500-539 and 33 70 49 38 700-743.

Operation

The wagon's deck height of 945mm from rail enables them to carry 9' 0" boxes on lines cleared for the W9 loading gauge or 9' 6" when some Intermodal routes are upgraded to the W12 loading gauge. This makes an interesting contrast with the 'Megafret' wagon which has its loading deck a mere 825mm above rail height. The IFA 'EuroTwins' are not restricted to international routes *via* the Channel Tunnel but also see use on a number of domestic flows.

A press release from EWS dated April 25, 2002, detailed their plans to operate 90mph Anglo-Scottish Intermodal services on the WCML, following successful night-time trials with the Intermodal fleet - assumed to be the 49 38 000-224 series of wagons. On September 24, 2002, EWS operated the first 90mph intermodal trial service for P&O Nedlloyd, reaching Mossend in just over five and a half hours of leaving Willesden. This had obvious implications for a variety of domestic traffic flows including containerised mail, perishable goods and 'just in time' distribution.

The Bachmann model

The model is superbly finished, with an even application of paint on the wagon itself and the printing on the container nothing short of excellent. The stunning thing about the model is the number of individually fitted parts, the fine quality printing of data panels, and application of yellow to the securing lugs. It is a pity to line up an airbrush filled with

track coloured paint to blast a bit of weathering over it!

The good mass of the wagon is achieved by die casting the central spine in metal and providing a screw fixing system for the wagon deck. Turning the model over (one of the twin-sets anyway) I was immediately taken by the superb fittings, brake cylinders - two of them - and an air receiving tank; all are individually fitted.

An empty set would look just as impressive on a layout as one loaded with containers - it's almost a pity to hide all that detail under a container! The twist-lock spigots are provided in a plastic bag for addition by the modeller. This is necessary because they are moved to suit the twist lock holes in the containers. Turning the wagon upright, the modelling of the top of the deck is very refined, complete with all the lugs and bracing.

The bogies are correct representations of the Y33 type, with 10mm diameter wheels of excellent quality - if you are a OO gauge modeller, the wheels will be more than adequate. Fitting closer-to-scale wheels to the bogies was a tight squeeze, as the spacing between the frames is 22mm. P4 modellers will be disappointed to see that they will need to make some modifications to ensure a good fit. The model is equipped with a close-coupling system that activates when the model rounds a curve. The cam mechanism is linked to the bogie spacer and this will push the coupling arm round and out to widen the spacing between wagons. The return spring is located discreetly under the model and not visible when it is loaded with a container. NEM-362 coupling pockets are provided that will accept the fishtail ended coupling bar provided with the wagon, or Kadee couplers Nos.17-19. I thought that the coupling bar for the inner coupling was a tad long and decided to shorten it on my models. The NEM-362 coupler pockets were mounted at the correct height and work very well with all NEM compatible couplings. An excellent adoption of a recognised standard.

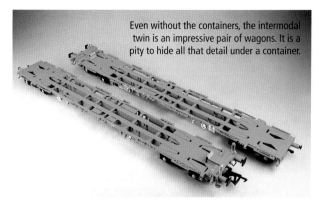

Even without the containers, the intermodal twin is an impressive pair of wagons. It is a pity to hide all that detail under a container.

Bachmann supplies its IFA wagons with two 45' containers or between two and four 20' boxes. This picture shows the model with 45' 'Seawheel' boxes of 13.7m x 2.5m.

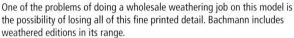

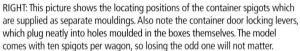

One of the problems of doing a wholesale weathering job on this model is the possibility of losing all of this fine printed detail. Bachmann includes weathered editions in its range.

RIGHT: This picture shows the locating positions of the container spigots which are supplied as separate mouldings. Also note the container door locking levers, which plug neatly into holes moulded in the boxes themselves. The model comes with ten spigots per wagon, so losing the odd one will not matter.

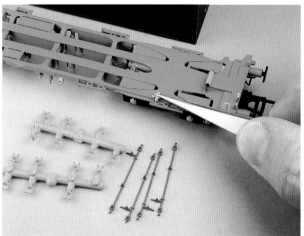

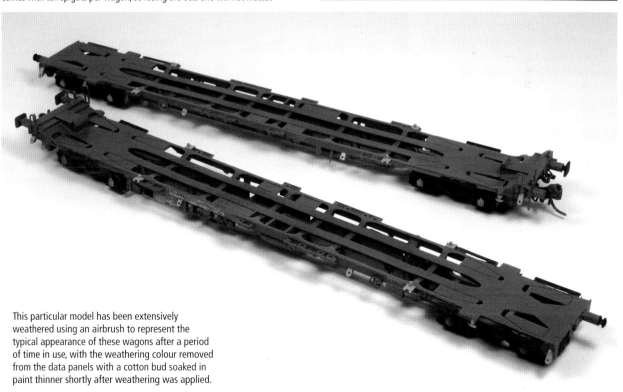

This particular model has been extensively weathered using an airbrush to represent the typical appearance of these wagons after a period of time in use, with the weathering colour removed from the data panels with a cotton bud soaked in paint thinner shortly after weathering was applied.

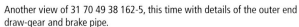

A single 'EuroTwin' set (IFA/FIA No.31 70 49 38 162-5) stopped for repair at Inverness Millburn Yard on August 21, 2002. The coating of grime completely hides the original body colour, which in this case was believed to be black. Note the square shank buffers and small fittings such as footsteps and handrails.

Close up view of the inner end coupling and buffer arrangement of IFA/FIA 31 70 49 38 162-5. Note the solid bar-type coupling with facility for separating the wagon. Notably, the inner buffers have a round shank with a flat surface on the underside, although the buffers fitted to the Bachmann model do not resemble this shape.

RIGHT: This view confirms the number - dirt almost obscures the data panels. The deck height of 945mm is achieved with Y33 small wheel bogies.

Brawa HO scale Sffggmrrss wagons

AAE is an international leasing company specialising in freight wagons and as far as modellers in Europe are concerned, it is well-known for its large fleet of Sffggmrrss 'Megafret' twin container wagons, which are seen widely in Europe and the UK on scheduled intermodal services. They have a loading deck 825mm from the rail, which means that they can, theoretically, be used with Hi-Cube containers on some UK routes. The AAE Sffggmrrss wagons have appeared on intermodal services in the UK, operated by various freight companies including DRS, which now operates a large fleet for its intermodal services from

Scotland to Daventry and from Grangemouth to Aberdeen and Elderslie near Glasgow. They are becoming closely associated with supermarket intermodal traffic for Asda and Tesco and have found use on the trial weekly intermodal service to Elgin that ran for six weeks in 2008.

Sffggmrrss wagons are characterised by having a low deck and bogies equipped with small wheels, resulting in a design of wagon that can make maximum use of the available loading gauge. Each platform has a useful loading length of 50' and a payload capacity of around 43t. They are capable of carrying containers from 20' to 45' in length and other intermodal units such as swap bodies and special containers

up to 49' in length.

At this point, it is worth noting that EWS operates a fleet of similar Sffggmrrss container wagons (TOPS coded FKA) which were constructed by Thrall. These can be distinguished from the AAE fleet by their colour, which is EWS maroon with EWS lettering, together with the registration numbers in the 81 70 4908 000-149 number sequence. They are 37720mm in length over the buffers, which is longer than the AAE Sffggmrrss wagons. They have detail differences in the position of brake equipment and the shape of the headstocks. It pays to observe wagon details when on the lineside! EWS also operates the blue AAE type.

The model

The only model currently available that would even be remotely suitable for modelling UK intermodal operations is the Brawa version of the Sffggmrrss' although Dapol announced one for British N gauge (1:148 scale) together with containers branded for Tesco traffic to go with its DRS Class 66/4 model. I looked at the Brawa HO model, which is supplied as a twin-set loaded with containers and pondered on whether it can be used as a stop-gap on 4mm scale layouts, in the hope that a ready-to-run British OO gauge model may be offered in the future by some enterprising manufacturer.

The Brawa model is very fine indeed, with well-defined detail. Printed livery details are very crisp and legible with no sign of fudging or blurring. There are a large number of separately fitted details such as brake pipe runs, brake equipment, handrails and brake wheels. I searched for tooling flash on all of the components and failed to find any, an indication of the high quality of this model. However, that quality comes at a price and you should not expect to pay much less than £75.00 per pair.

The bogies are commendably fine and come complete with brake blocks aligned with the wheels and perfectly concentric wheels of 7.7mm diameter which is a tad undersize when compared to the prototype. The wheels themselves are equipped with pinpoint axles of 24mm length and have a width of 3.2mm which is quite coarse. The bogies themselves are fixed with a small crosshead screw, which is screwed into a metal collar fitted to the model. This should prevent the pivot hole from becoming stripped of its thread should the model suffer rough handling.

Each twin is permanently coupled together using the same screw and mounting pivot on the inner bogies to secure a fixed coupling bar. To enable the model to operate around sharp curves, the detail on the inner end of each wagon is not quite correct when compared to photographs of the prototype. The outer ends are equipped with a NEM coupling pocket which is fitted to a spacing mechanism, that enables the wagon to negotiate sharp curves, yet remain close coupled when on the straight. Kadee users will be pleased to know that the NEM coupling pocket is fitted to the specified height for use with No. 19 Kadees. It is worth noting that the model is supplied with a continental style loop coupling which is designed to fit the NEM coupling pocket.

The example shown here was loaded with four 20' containers with various modern shipping company liveries, including P&O Nedlloyd and Maersk. Examining the containers closely, I suspect that they are based on older designs because there are details which do not match my own photographic records of containers used by those companies. Each container is clipped firmly to the underframe with simple spigots moulded on the floor of each container. This does not affect the appearance of the container securing lugs moulded to the side of the wagon.

The model was tested on both an HO and a OO gauge layout and was found to be free running and reliable through a variety of different pointwork. It was a little strange to watch the wagon in operation without its containers because the deck was barely higher than the platform height on a UK-outline layout and the large holes in the floor of the wagon meant that you could see rather more of the track than you might expect!

I experimented by loading the model with a pair of Bachmann 4mm scale 45' containers to see if it is possible to use this model as a compromise on a OO gauge layout, in an effort to replicate DRS intermodal traffic. This is spurred by the availability of transfers for Malcom Logistic Services livery to suit

The Brawa 'Megafret' wagon model is offered as a semi permanently coupled twin set with containers. Brawa has offered three different versions of the model featuring different containers.

Table 3: AAE Sffggmrrss leading dimensions 1:87.1 scale, HO gauge

Dimension	Prototype (mm)	Scale (mm)	Model (mm)
Length over buffers	36,440	418	418
Bogie centres	13,080	150	150
Outer platform length	2,300	26.5	26
Inner platform length	1,900	22	22
Inner coupling space	640	7.3	8
Wheelbase of bogie	2,000	23	23
Deck height from rail	825	9.5	9.5
Buffer height	1,025	11.8	11.8
Wheel diameter	730	8.4	7.7

Note: The model is classified by Brawa as Epoch V – circa 1990 to present day, although actual introduction dates for specific wagons will vary.

the 45' box (by C-Rail Intermodal). The 45' box will fit the model's loading deck without overhanging the inner end, although it is difficult to match the twist-lock holes on the container with the container lugs on the wagon. As you would expect, the container overhung the sides of the wagon a little more than would be cosmetically acceptable. To be honest, I thought the containers overwhelmed the model considerably more than expected.

Nonetheless, HO modellers can enjoy this lovely model, especially if run with an HO scale Class 66 such as the lovely DCC sound equipped model from Mehano. You could have a basis for an interesting project as a result. For British HO scale, all you need is some HO scale transfers to suit the Mehano Class 66 to redress it as a British locomotive, although Mehano does not currently offer the low emission version.

Dimensions

I examined the model and compared its leading dimensions with those published by AAE in its technical literature. I found that the model was within 0.5mm in most respects and for the majority of the leading dimensions, it was spot on – there are no dimensional errors that would cause a problem. Table 3 shows the comparison between prototype and the 1:87.1 scale model.

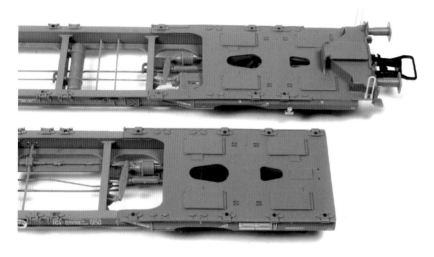

Fine detail is not restricted to the underframe components, it may also be found on the loading deck of the wagon and the representation of the container securing points.

Making the best of the Bachmann 20' container

C-Rail Intermodal offers the correct paint colours to complement the

Experiments with 4mm scale Bachmann 45' containers were made to establish if this model could be used as a stand-in on British outline layouts.

Although the Bachmann container fits on the loading deck of the wagon (just!), it does tend to overwhelm it.

Asda 45′ containers are conveyed in DRS intermodal services on the West Coast Main Line, usually loaded on 'Megafret' wagons. This one was photographed at Carlisle on September 18, 2006. The wagon was Sffggmrrss No. 33 68 4909 456, an AAE lease wagon. The container livery has been offered by Bachmann as part of its 2007 releases.

specially commissioned transfers from Microscale intended for Bachmann standard 20′ ISO boxes. Numerous colours are available in gloss to suit the needs of 4mm scale modellers including OOCL, P&O, Evergreen, Hapag-Lloyd, MSC and Genstar, offering a little colour to the intermodal scene. The transfers themselves were checked for accuracy using the company websites for reference.

ISO containers are heavily ribbed and as such present a challenge for the application of transfers. Two setting solutions from the Microscale decals range should be used to soften the transfers and enable them to sit onto the model without bridging the space between ribs. It is perhaps fortunate that the paint colours (produced by Phoenix Precision) are now gloss because the ideal surface to apply Microscale transfers is one with a gloss finish. Adhesion of the transfers is very good on a gloss finish and the carrier film will be completely hidden.

The choice of shipping line names now available from C-Rail Intermodal is well considered. OOCL, P&O Hapag Lloyd and Mitsui OSK Lines are names

British intermodal enthusiasts are beginning to enjoy some good trade support. Products are now available from Bachmann, Dapol, Heljan, C-Rail Intermodal, S Kits and Genesis Kits. That includes a handful of wagons, a variety of containers, paints and transfers. However, there is a long way to go before UK outline modellers can model intermodal operations to the same level as their US counterparts in any scale. The popularity of intermodal operations is down to the wide variety of containers and wagons used on this type of traffic together with a colourful selection of liveries. This ad hoc selection of products demonstrates how colourful intermodal modelling can be.

frequently seen on Freightliner and EWS intermodal services. Some of the boxes represented by the Bachmann model are not so common except perhaps the superb P&O boxes supplied with one of its Intermodal twin wagons.

The C-Rail commissioned Intermodal transfers and paints immediately offer many different colours and names to bring added authenticity to trains made up of container wagons, or scenes with stacked containers.

1. C-RAIL Intermodal commissions paints from Phoenix Precision to complement transfers for container liveries, available in 2 and 4mm scales. The paint is now gloss in finish, which will accept waterslide transfers without carrier film ghosts.
2. Removing the door locking rods from the Bachmann 20' boxes was a struggle. So much glue

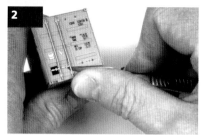

had been used to secure them that I wondered if they would ever budge without breaking. Bachmann could do much to help the modeller by providing undecorated containers for painting by the modeller – with the rods left off the model in the same manner as the 45' containers supplied with its intermodal wagon. C-Rail Intermodal offers

spare locking bars should you need them!
3. Gentle action with a fibre pencil removes the old container markings. I chose to repaint the grey containers for this project because grey makes an excellent base for the new colours. Each box is then thoroughly washed and left in a dust free place to dry before painting.

4. The transfers supplied by C-Rail Intermodal are produced by Microscale, a US based company which has a huge range of transfers for US outline models. Microscale offers a complete transfer finishing system for its waterslide transfers. Setting solutions are available to make the transfers sit onto irregular surfaces without bridging the ribs or other detail. In this case, the setting solution is brushed onto the model and then the transfer floated into place.

The transfer softens and more readily takes the shape of the surface when treated with setting solutions. Excess water and solution is dabbed away with absorbent kitchen paper. Leave the transfer to dry thoroughly once it is in place. Any transfer that is still bridging detail can be further treated with setting solution but only after the first application has dried.
5. Finished containers grace the Bachmann IFA intermodal twin wagon.

To achieve real authenticity, this collection of re-decorated containers should be weathered, especially around the twist-lock holes where rust is common. Any point on a container that makes contact with other containers, wagons or the ground soon looses its paint. Maritime conditions also takes their toll on container paint finishes.

Modelling 'standard' 40' containers from a kit

One of the prominent missing links in the modelling of standard ISO containers was also the most unlikely, because the 40' container is perhaps the most common box of them all. I find it strange that Bachmann should have chosen the extended 45' box to go with its IFA intermodal model when a 40' by 2.5 metre or 45' by 8' 6" container would have been the more logical choice. Construction of the C-Rail 40' box kit is very straightforward requiring only simple tools and a solvent cement suitable for styrene plastic to assemble it.

Whilst the construction of the containers is straightforward, finishing them requires a little more skill. The ribbed surfaces on standard containers makes it a little more challenging to apply large transfers, as described opposite on page 108. If the model is finished with gloss varnish prior to the application of transfers then it will be much easier to disguise the carrier film and achieve a good bond between the surface of the model and the transfer itself. I found that construction time accounted for 20 minutes per box. Finishing time after painting and varnishing took about an hour per box to get a perfect seamless finish between the paint and the transfers. Remember, the aim is to make your transfers appear as if they were painted on.

 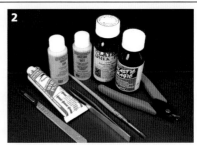

1. C-Rail Intermodal 40' container kit and matching waterslide transfers. Painting your containers in authentic company liveries is straightforward because C-Rail Intermodal also offers the correct paint colours to match its transfers.
2. Some of the tools and materials used use to assemble and finish C-Rail Intermodal container kits are shown here. The tools themselves are very basic and every modeller is likely to have them to hand. The exception may be the Xuron cutters, which are designed to easily and safely remove plastic kit parts from the sprue. They save a great deal of money in avoiding the blunting of your modelling knife blades.

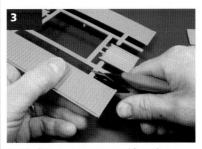 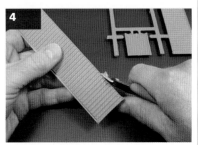

3. All of the parts are removed from the sprue with Xuron plastic sprue cutters. Start by cutting each sprue in the middle rather than at the edge of each part. Sometimes, it is not easy to place the cutting blades right up to the required finished edge until the sprue is broken down into individual parts.
4. Follow up by removing the remnant of the sprue with the cutters, now it is easier to get at the finished edge. The resulting cut is usually sharp and requires minimal filing to clean up the edge.

 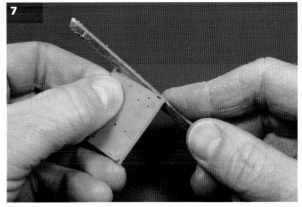

6. Gently file away any sprue that remains together with feed points and moulding flash. In the main this kit was clean, requiring minimal cleaning with a file.
7. More filing and cleaning of the container ends.

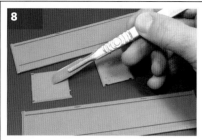

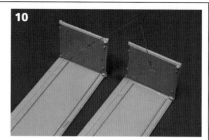

8. The kit parts are orientated. Follow the assembly instructions carefully because each container end is identified with a letter that corresponds to the same letter moulded at the end of each side. The letter is clearly moulded on the inside face of each part.

9. Plastic solvent cement is applied to each join - sparingly - to avoid flooding the model.

10. Note that the ends have been glued to the corresponding end of the container side identified with either the letter B or F. Don't get them the wrong way round!

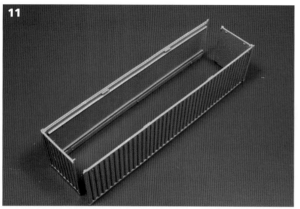

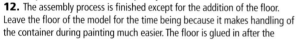

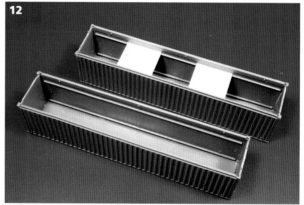

11. The container is assembled as two halves and brought together after the first joins have hardened completely.

12. The assembly process is finished except for the addition of the floor. Leave the floor of the model for the time being because it makes handling of the container during painting much easier. The floor is glued in after the container has been completely finished with transfers and varnish. The separately moulded door locking bars are also added at the end of the finishing process. The container can be strengthened by temporarily inserting pieces of styrene or the floor, as shown in this picture. They prevent the sides from bowing inwards until the floor piece is permanently fitted.

The C-Rail Intermodal container kits are most welcome, being easy to assemble and interesting to finish, thanks to excellent product support with paint and transfers. They fit both the Genesis Kits intermodal wagon kits and the Bachmann IFA twin intermodal wagon, the locking bar positions in the kit being a perfect match. Any modeller that has had to contend with broken door locking bars on their Bachmann 20' containers can buy the door locking bar moulding from this kit as a separate item. It was designed with the same measurements as those used on the Bachmann containers.

Modelling 30' bulk containers

Further intermodal colour and variety is available in the form of a 30' 'Bulktainer' kit from C-Rail Intermodal which is an ideal companion for the superb Bachmann Intermodal twin. The modelled container is one of three types that have been used for bulk commodities such as plastic pellets and other similar products. This 'Bulktainer' represents the 8' 6" high version at 2.5 metres wide. The latest designs are 9' in height. The company has given thought to finishing the container and provides two sheets of decals sufficient to complete more than one 'Bulktainer': One sheet has two IBC and one UBC transfer sets whilst the other has sufficient for four IFF registered 'Bulktainers'. Appropriate paint colours are produced by Phoenix Precision and are available from C-Rail Intermodal.

They can be assembled in about an hour of careful work and there is no reason why the bulk pack of five kits could not keep you happily occupied

The finished result sits on the back of an IFA. The containers lock on to the locking spigots quite securely and no other method of holding the containers in place is required.

for an evening, with assembly made on a modelling tray in front of the television! The biggest challenge in completing one of these kits is application of the large transfers, which have an extensive area of carrier film which must be blended into the paint scheme, so that the transfers themselves give the impression of being painted on. Once again, Microscale Decal Set

and Decal Sol solutions will enable you to place the transfers correctly and bed them in to the highly irregular surface of the model. It is worth noting that the transfers intended for the kit are a tad on the large side, being correctly sized for the 9' version. Nonetheless, they can be positioned with care to minimise the impact and the final appearance is impressive.

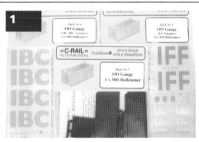

1. New products from C-Rail Intermodal include the 30' 'Bulktainer' and transfers for companies that operate them including UBC and IFF. The transfers are commissioned from Microscale.

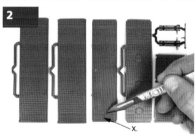

2. The container is a simple kit moulded from styrene plastic which is easily assembled with liquid poly cement. Look out for the letter X moulded in the floor and top panel. This denotes the end to which the container door panel is

assembled.
3. Wet and dry paper can be used to gently smooth any rough edges before assembly, instead of a file as shown with the construction of the 40' box earlier in the chapter.

4. The ends and roof are assembled together first, using sparing amounts of liquid poly cement.
5. Sides are assembled to the roof and

ends sub-assembly. Ensuring that you fit the door panel to the parts marked with an 'X' is important for a close fit.

6. This image illustrates how the spigots moulded to the end panels are designed to give a positive lock to the container roof.

7. Liquid poly cement should be applied sparingly to the inside of the model and the floor left to one side until you are sure that all traces of solvent have evaporated.

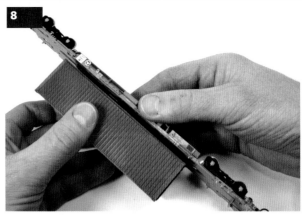

8. The container can be test fitted to a Bachmann Intermodal wagon prior to painting. It locks onto those tiny yellow container lock mouldings accurately and securely.

Bachmann 45 foot containers make an interesting contrast with the C-Rail Intermodal 'Bulktainer'. The latter looks at home on the back of the Bachmann IFA model which is just as well because 'Bulktainers' are commonly seen on EWS Intermodal services.

20' container tank

C-Rail Intermodal also include a 20'container tank of a common design used throughout the logistics industry within its catalogue. It may be quickly assembled as supplied using liquid poly cement or used as a basis for kit bashing into one of the other types of container tanks of which there are many. The modeller would have to be prepared to put some research into these containers because very little published information exists. Container tanks generally carry the liveries of their owning shipping company and, as a result, could be seen on almost any intermodal train carrying one of a variety of liquid products from chemicals to foodstuffs. One of the reasons why trains of liquid chemical tank wagons have all but disappeared from the network is that many industrial companies now prefer the flexibility of container tanks. Only the presence of hazchem markings will betray the container's contents.

The kit is supported with transfers, enabling the modeller to choose one of the variety of shipping companies liveries including Bulkhaul, Stolt, Suttons and Seabrook. The transfers are available on two sheets: Pack 14 for two types of Bulkhaul markings and Pack 19 for the remainder, including a variety of hazchem markings for various chemicals. The transfers are produced for C-Rail Intermodal by Microscale and are compatible with Microscale's setting solutions.

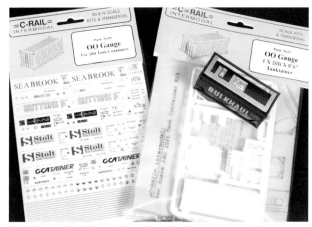

C-Rail Intermodal offers a wide variety of products to support the Intermodal modeller in 2mm and 4mm scale. Usually, when they produce a kit, the transfers are also commissioned. This is the case with its 20' container tank.

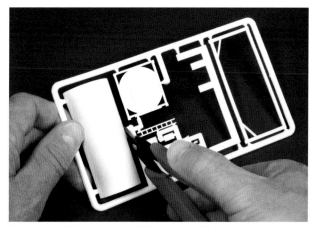

Construction of the container tank kit is very straightforward, although some care must be taken to prevent the frame from warping. Sprue cutters neatly remove parts from the fret as they are needed. The tank barrel is assembled first.

The sparing use of solvent cement should help to avoid any distortion of the delicate side members, which are shown assembled, together with the tank ends. Note that the joins in the tank barrel are off-set so the top join will be hidden under the walkway and the bottom one hidden behind the framing. This saves the need to spend valuable modelling time finishing the joins so they will not show through the paint.

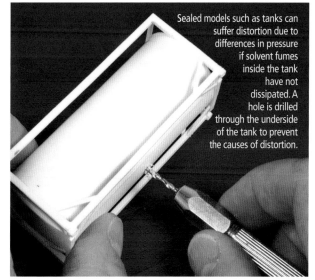

Sealed models such as tanks can suffer distortion due to differences in pressure if solvent fumes inside the tank have not dissipated. A hole is drilled through the underside of the tank to prevent the causes of distortion.

The plastic walkway does cover the barrel join very nicely.

Some details are not added to the model until they have been painted. It is much easier to paint them off the model than having to painstakingly paint them on the model. Those details include the filler hatch details and walkways which should be painted a stainless steel colour.

ABOVE: Grangemouth is an increasingly busy location for freight traffic and that includes intermodal traffic from Europe *via* Trafford Park hauled by EWS and block trains of supermarket containers hauled by DRS. DRS also operates mixed intermodal trains from Grangemouth to Aberdeen for Asda and Malcom Logistics together with trains for Daventry for the same companies and Russells. EWS runs mixed intermodal trains as can be seen on the left of the picture. The train on the right is the Grangemouth-Daventry Tesco service.

LEFT: A trial service that commenced in 2008 for six weeks was a weekly intermodal from Elgin carrying boxes and tanks for McPherson Ltd. of Aberlour. This picture shows the trial service pausing at Nairn to surrender the Forres-Nairn single line token on May 30, 2008. Not all modern intermodal services are hauled by Class 66s as this service was booked to run with Class 67s between Inverness and Elgin.

ABOVE: A shortage of motive power and failures can lead to locomotives from other operators being used on scheduled services. Freightliner regularly hires DRS traction for some of its services as was seen at Burton-on-Trent on June 7, 2008.

RIGHT: EWS is heavily involved in intermodal container operations thanks to it inheriting the European traffic from Railfreight Distribution. It invested in further wagons that could be used on intermodal operations including the Thrall-built FAA low-deck and FCA spines in addition to the Euro-twins. Class 92s are frequently used on the WCML on the Grangemouth-Trafford Park services as seen on the evening of June 5, 2008 when 92 034 paused for a crew change.

BELOW: A diverted Felixstowe-Hams Hall intermodal passes Burton-on-Trent on June 7, 2008 with GBRf Class 66, No.66 723 in charge. Note the MSC boxes, for which transfers and paint are available. Also, Bachmann has offered its 20' box in MSC colours.

LEFT: There are no examples of the first truly modern intermodal wagon still operating today. The original Freightliner FFA/FGA sets have seen 40 years of service. Despite this, there is no scale model available at the time of writing in the summer of 2008 even though there are rumours of an off-the-shelf model from one of the mainstream manufacturers.

BELOW: The only ready-to-run option for modelling the FFA and FGA was to purchase the elderly Hornby model and apply a detailing kit from S Kits to upgrade it.

Freightliner FSA wagon No.608404 passes Didcot station on the avoiding lines in the formation of a northbound Freightliner working from Southampton. Note the difference in colour between the two P&O boxes which means that it's not always critical to obtain an exact paint match when painting containers. The maritime shipping environment is harsh on paint and boxes alike. A 20' container is available from Bachmann. The 40' box can be modelled using the new kit from C-Rail Intermodal.

This portrait of a Freightliner-operated FEA-B wagon loaded with a 40' and a 20'container was taken at Millbrook in December 2003. Freightliner also operates a single version of this wagon. Dapol was expected to release its OO gauge model of the FEA-B in 2008.

You have a better chance of modelling some of the EWS intermodal operations thanks to the Bachmann IFA EuroTwin model and its Class 66 model together with good trade support from C-Rail Intermodal. The 30' 'Bulktainer' seen in this view taken at Carlisle in June 2005 is available as a simple plastic kit together with transfers and paint.

This is another version of a 'Bulktainer' now commonly seen on EWS intermodal services and easily modelled in 4mm scale. 'Bulktainers' are used to convey a variety of granular materials in bulk, such as sand, plastic pellets and road salt to mention a few. In the past, these products may have been conveyed in specialist covered hoppers which have disappeared from the rail network. The disappearance of those wagon types does not necessarily mean that the traffic has been lost to rail, simply the mode of transportation has changed.

A 30' 'Bulktainer' in IFF livery.

A Sffggmrrss 'Megafret' twin container wagon.

It is possible to model MSC boxes using products from C-Rail Intermodal. FEA-A No.630004 is another version of the FEA, the FEA-A which finds use in GBRf intermodal services as well as Gypsum traffic. Note the fold up container locating pedestals. FEAs have been built in large numbers for intermodal and an engineers' version of it which involves the use of modules. FEAs are becoming a large subject for wagon modellers to investigate.

Hapag Lloyd containers loaded on a Freightliner FSA wagon.

Very little of this everyday scene depicted in this picture of Southampton Maritime can be modelled in 4mm scale using off-the-shelf products. Yet this is a typical and rapidly growing sphere of railway operation. Nonetheless, operational container cranes with Digital Command Control are available from Heljan and manufacturers are, as of 2008, waking up to the potential of intermodal markets with suggestion of new containers and wagons. However, this does not complete the scene as can be seen in this picture. Pup trailers, tractor units and road vehicles together with a host of other related equipment represent opportunities for manufacturers yet to be exploited.

'EuroTwin' IFA No.33 70 4938 705-9 brings up the rear with a 20' box and a 20' tank at Nuneaton on June 29, 2002. This wagon is painted in green under all the brake dust and grime. The running number applies to each twin-set and not the individual wagon.

Container tanks loaded on IFA 33 70 4938 733-1, at Nuneaton on June 29, 2002. Container tanks are particularly attractive yet no reasonable off-the-shelf 4mm scale model exists to date. Modellers wishing to determine where all the yellow brackets supplied with the Bachmann IFA model are located can use this view to see how the container lugs are fitted to the wagon and adjusted depending on container length.

LEFT: Deep-sea container terminal operations such as this seen at Southampton Maritime are challenging to model accurately in 4mm scale without resorting to a great deal of scratch-building or using products from abroad, which may be manufactured to 1:87 scale. However, kits for containers and tanks together with appropriate transfers and paints have been made available from C-Rail Intermodal for some time, including 40' boxes and transfers to model the OOCL containers seen here. When looking at modelling containers, be aware of the difference in height as well as length!

Bachmann's new air-braked open wagon maodels, which include the OBA and OCA, present some interesting opportunities for simple customisation. Take OBA No. 110472 for example. Signs of 'SatLink' livery remain on the ends, whilst the wooden drop doors are a patchwork of new planks in plain wood and EWS maroon paint.

Until recently, and despite the longevity of the long wheelbase air-braked wagon designs associated with the BR Railfreight era, the only route to a half way decent model of the OBA, OCA and SPA was to construct the plastic kits by Cambrian Models, which were not without their challenges. Vans were not available, except the reasonable but old Hornby VDA model which could be used as a base for modelling VAA, VBA and VCA vans using etched sides. That too was not without issues of accuracy, together with having to make use of a dated underframe design. Finally, the OAA 'Open AB' wagons remains in the Hornby catalogue, a model which is dated and would benefit from new tooling.

Mention should be made of the larger, almost continental-style VGA (VKA) sliding-wall van which was an earlier wagon model produced by Bachmann which filled an important gap for many modellers and still available today. With regard to the majority of air-braked opens and vans, it's taken until around 2007 to see reasonably accurate models of some, if not all of the classic Railfreight wagons become widely available off-the-shelf, largely thanks to Bachmann. At the time of writing, the OBA, OCA, VAA, VAB, VBA and VGA are available. The proposed Bachmann VDA van is still to make an appearance at the time of writing, but is expected to have the same axleguard arrangement as the other Bachmann wagons of this family. There appears to be no plans for an SPA plate and wire carrying wagon, nor variations on the underframes, such as timber (ex-VDA) and spoil and ballast wagons (ex-OBA and OCA). The SPA can still be modelled from the Cambrian Models kit and the various re-bodied ballast/spoil wagons constructed on the Bachmann underframes; both projects are, however, beyond the scope of this book.

It is unfortunate that Bachmann have adopted a pivoting axleguard arrangement so that their wagons will negotiate train set curves. This causes problems for Kadee coupler users, as the swing coupling mount does not always align the coupling with the adjacent wagon's coupling. Finescale modellers using closer-to-scale wheels will find that road-holding is not what it should be. This chapter will look at making improvements to the Bachmann wagons including the following:

- Removal of the pivoting axleguards and replacing them with fixed etched ones capable of accepting 26mm length axles, and closer to scale wheels on the OBA and OCA
- Adding more detailed suspension and axleboxes
- Demonstrating the use of sprung suspension axleguards to improve performance on both opens and vans
- Converting the Bachmann ventilated van to a non-ventilated type
- Improving the fit of the NEM coupling pockets for use with Kadee couplers and tension lock couplings
- Painting and weathering techniques to represent battered and used wagons are described in Chapter 10

THE MODELS
The OBA

OBAs are modern air-braked five-plank wagons constructed in two batches between 1977 and 1980. The first batch

Bachmann had released four versions of the VAA/VBA van at the time when this book was being compiled, three of which are shown here: No. 200116 in Railfreight grey livery, No. 200241 in EWS livery together with No. 200289 in BR bauxite livery without Railfreight markings.

Bachmann released three versions of its new OCA 31.5t air braked open wagon in 2007.

was built at Ashford on a new design of underframe with a 6,320mm wheelbase and fitted with leaf springs, which were replaced with Bruninghaus springs at a later date to enable running at higher speeds. The second batch built at Shildon were thus equipped from new

and this is the version represented by the Bachmann model of the OBA. The body features high ends compared to the bodyside doors, of which there are four, with removable stanchions. The first wagons were painted maroon, a livery superseded by Railfreight red

Bachmann offers one version of its OCA model in original Railfreight red colours. Closer inspection reveals that it is adorned with post-1998 electrification warning notices and has maroon painted axleboxes which would be consistent with EWS ownership. The model is characterised by having body sides which are far too thick and the top edge of the body sides and ends are too smooth, lacking detail which would otherwise represent the drop side door and stanchion frames.

A typical VBA van is represented by the new Bachmann model, one of which is finished in EWS livery as No.200241.

and grey colours. Interestingly enough, the OBA has come full circle, as many can be found in maroon once again, this time painted in the EWS version of the colour.

In recent times, OBAs used on block traffic have been equipped with extensions to their ends and fitting of mesh doors in place of the wooden ones. The most recent conversions were undertaken at Warrington Arpley in 2008. They are used on a variety of traffic, from departmental duties, including material recovery from works sites, block traffic (using the similar OAAs from the Mendips to Acton, which have also been equipped with mesh doors as replacements for the planked ones) and block traffic from Heck in Yorkshire. Wagons used on block traffic have been painted in a variety of liveries including 'Plasmor Blockfreight' colours and a mixture of patch painting efforts as modifications have been undertaken.

The majority of OBAs found employment in departmental use under BR, being recoded ZDA and coded 'Bass'. Many were painted in engineers' yellow/grey livery as a result and ran in those colours for many years. It was not unusual to see new, unpainted planks fitted to the OBAs and ZDAs as repairs were undertaken. As usual, reference photographs will help with livery details and also modifications, such as extensions to the wagon ends.

The Bachmann model features rotating axleguards, which are replaced with sprung ones later in the chapter. The body moulding appears to be pretty good, except that the sides are too thick. The underframe is good, once those axleguards have been dealt with and the coupling arrangement revised. Bachmann has offered the model in several guises: original Railfreight colours, a block wagon with extended ends, an EWS version equipped with extended ends and in original condition but decorated in EWS livery.

The long wheelbase sliding wall van remains a popular model in the Bachmann catalogue. It too features pivoting axleguards which can result in less than perfect running.

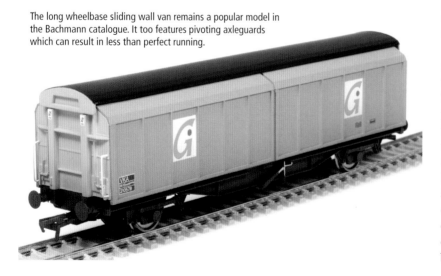

Table 1: Overall dimensional accuracy of the Bachmann OBA

Dimensions	Actual (mm)	Scale (mm)	Model (mm)	Difference (mm)
Length over buffers	11,430	150	150	0
Length over body	10,670	140	140	0
Length over headstocks	10,450	137	139	+2
Inside length	10,438	137	136	-1
Inside width	2,339	30.5	28.5	-2
Wheelbase	6,320	83	83	0
Height from rail	2,280	30	30	0
Height of body	1,000	13	13	0
Wheel diameter	915	12	12.5	+0.5

Table 2: Overall dimensional accuracy of the Bachmann OCA

Dimensions	Actual (mm)	Scale (mm)	Model (mm)	Difference (mm)
Length over buffers	11,430	150	150	0
Length over body	10,670	140	142	+2
Length over headstocks	10,450	137	137	0
Inside length	10,438	137	135	-2
Extreme width	2,550	33.5	33.5	0
Inside width	2,339	30.5	29	-1.5
Wheelbase	6,320	83	83	0
Height from rail	2,203	29	29	0
Height of body	915	12	12	0
Wheel diameter	915	12	12.5	+0.5

The OCA

BR introduced the OCA 31.5tonne air-braked general open wagon between 1981 and 1982. They were constructed at Shildon to the same overall dimensions as the OBA but with a new underframe and featuring an all-steel design with three drop-side doors per side, removable stanchions between them, fixed steel ends and turnover bolsters built into a wooden floor. The chassis was fitted with Bruninghaus suspension springs from new. 400 wagons were built in total in one lot to design code OC001A and numbered in the air-braked wagon series 112000-112399. All 400 wagons were finished in Railfreight red. Not all remain in traffic in their original form, because some redundant OCAs have been re-bodied to create ZCA 'Sea Horse' ballast wagons and various types of OTA timber wagons, all of which would make interesting projects using the Bachmann model as a starting point.

Taking a look at the model, the chassis is equipped with many factory applied details, including brake levers, brake actuation equipment, air tanks and distributor. Noteworthy on this model is the use of separate pivoting axleguard mouldings which are designed to help the model negotiate sharp set-track curves. The coupling boxes are moulded as part of the axleguards which means that they pivot too. This was found to be an awkward arrangement when it came to accurate coupling and uncoupling of wagons during shunting moves.

By today's standards of tooling, the body moulding can be described as 'chunky' because the sides and ends are considerably wider than scale. On one hand, the thick plastic sides do much to prevent them from bowing inwards at the price of a finer appearance. But on the other, the overall appearance of the model is compromised by this chunky aspect of the body. The over-width sides are reflected in the figures in Table 2, where the inside width and length of the model are less than the scale measurements taken from the prototype.

Internally, the floor is correctly moulded, with planking and impressions of turnover bolsters. The top edge of the body has no definition to show that it is equipped with three drop-side doors on each side together with removable door stanchions.

Railfreight vans

Bachmann added two versions of the 1969-1970 COV AB van in 2008, the VAA and VBA with conventional non-ventilated body and the rarer ventilated type, of which only 20 were constructed. The VDA van model was still in development at the time of writing.

This type of wagon is still in traffic

today, albeit in reduced numbers and they can be seen in a variety of liveries, including Railfreight grey, but in very faded condition and without the original Railfreight markings. Some VAA/VBA vans were repainted in EWS livery and all livery variations since Railfreight grey and red livery can be found in MoD traffic. Some VAA/VBA vehicles were allocated to departmental duties and they can still be found dotted around the network today.

Bachmann has represented these vans reasonably well, using a new underframe which has potential for modelling several different types of wagon should Bachmann choose to investigate them further, including the OAA open wagon (with variations used in block traffic), the FPA container flat, the SAA steel bolster wagon and the more specialised VCA air-braked van.

The models measure up very well when compared to published drawings and appear to be of the correct length, width and of accurate proportions. It is worth noting that the almost imperceptible seams in the panelling, located on the ends of full-size VAA/VBA vans, has been over emphasised on the Bachmann model and some modellers may wish to smooth them away with a file and wet and dry paper. Conversely, the fine roof panel lines that

can be observed on the full-size vans are not present on the model.

Some of the underframe detail is not as well represented as it could be for a contemporary standard model and some modellers may object to the articulated axleguards too. There is no detail representing the disc brake calipers as a result and the brake push rodding on one side of the chassis is not accurate. However, this leaves the door open to some detailing and modification, which is described later in the chapter, including the fitting of fixed or sprung axleguards, replacement wheels with the correct representation of brake discs, additional brake rodding and upgraded airbrake equipment which can be purchased as castings from several small part manufacturers.

Transfers are available from Fox Transfers should renumbering and re-lettering of the wagons be desired. Looking at the variety of liveries which could be found on these vehicles, together with the colour fading that can be seen on the remaining vehicles today, there is a great deal of potential for modellers to make their mark by customising them with different weathering effects and the application of hazchem symbols. With a small amount of workshop time, they could be turned into a truly outstanding model.

The VGA/VKA sliding wall van

The VGA van model remains a popular wagon in the Bachmann catalogue. They remain in use today, earning their keep on a variety of services, including MoD traffic centred on Didcot where they are commonly found alongside VAA vans. The model is a fair representation of the prototype, with sharp tooling of the body, enhanced with separate handrails and other small details. The underframe is not as good as one might have hoped, because Bachmann have used the articulated axleguard arrangement so the model can negotiate sharp curves, in the same manner as the VAA and VBA.

In fact, this was Bachmann's first use of this method and it has been perpetuated in the newer air-braked wagon releases, despite feedback from the modeller asking for better definition in this area. This whole area of the model is the thing that lets it down a little; with chunky axlebox mouldings, undernourished suspension springs and the aforementioned axleguards which are too close together to accept wheels with 26mm axles, P4 wheels are a real push to fit, EM wheels squeeze in – just. The axleboxes need some careful preparation and fitting with pin point bearing cups to make them work.

Table 3: Summary of Railfreight vans and open wagons

TOPS code	Wagon type	Date built	Number sequence	Model manufacturer
OAA	31t Open (Wooden sides)	1971	100000-100099	Hornby
OBA	31t Open (Wooden sides)	1977-80	110001-110800	Bachmann
OCA	31t Open (Steel sides)	1981-82	11200-112399	Bachmann
VAA	29t Vanfit (Full length doors)	1969-70	200000-200208	Bachmann
VBA	24t Vanfit (Full length doors)	1970-71	200210-200324	Bachmann
VCA	24t Vanfit (Centre doors)	1971-74	200325-200549	None
VBA	24t Vanfit (Full length doors)	1974-75	200550-200649	Bachmann
VDA	24t Vanfit (Full length doors)	1976-78	200650-210399	Hornby Bachmann
VGA	28t sliding wall van	1983	201401-210650	Bachmann
SPA	31t plate wagon	1979-1981	460000-461101	Kit only

Note: Those former OBA, OCA, VCA and VDA wagons converted to different types including OTAs, runners, ZCAs, etc, retain the original wagon numbers making identification of a wagon's origins relatively straightforward. Also, there are gaps in number sequences as wagons have been disposed of or converted to other uses.

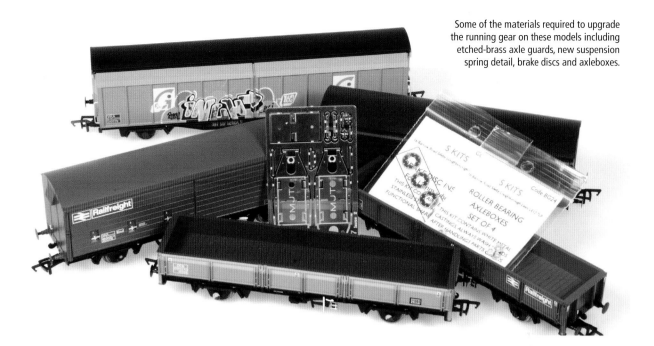

Some of the materials required to upgrade the running gear on these models including etched-brass axle guards, new suspension spring detail, brake discs and axleboxes.

The model has been released in a variety of liveries, including the original Railfreight red livery (colour was applied to the wagon ends whilst the wall doors were left unpainted) with Railfreight branding on panels placed on the doors. The use of such panels was quickly discontinued, especially when sector liveries emerged, resulting in the red being replaced by yellow. Subsequently, these wagons have borne EWS livery and several adaptations for the pre-privatisation companies such as Transrail and customer branding.

The model can be immediately improved by making the articulated axleguards fixed by either tightening the pivot screw or gluing them in place. This makes the van less able to round train set curves. On the positive side, this enables the couplings to engage correctly with those of adjacent wagons and improves the performance of the wagon over turnouts and crossings.

MODELLING PROJECTS
Upgrading the OCA wagon

This project shows the conversion of the Bachmann OCA model to improve the running gear with etched-brass axleguards and cast metal suspension details. The same work can be applied to the similar OBA model. Later in the chapter, the conversion to sprung suspension using Bill Bedford axleguards is demonstrated on the OBA model.

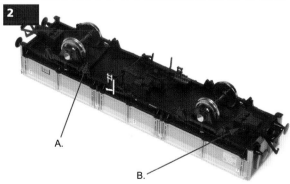

1. Whilst appearing strange, the angled yellow and blue paint applied to the axle boxes of the BR departmental version is correct for this wagon circa 2002. It is embellished with the later electrification warning notices.
2. The underframe features articulated axle guard assemblies (A) which include the coupling mounts with their NEM 362 coupling pockets (B). This is supposed to assist operation of the wagon on sharp 'set track' curves but in reality, a single axle arrangement like this does little to guide the model into curves, unlike a bogie with two axles.

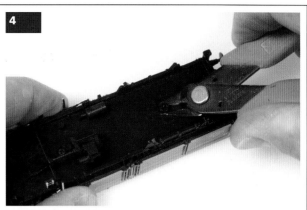

3. Each axleguard assembly is held in place with a single screw. Around 20 seconds' work and this is what we have. Note the pivot boss indicated by the red arrow.

4. Snip the pivot boss off if using fixed or compensated brass axleguards.

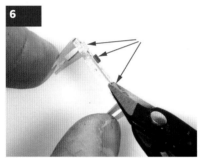

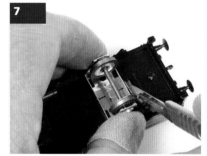

5. Pare away all raised detail to leave the floor flat.

6. The best representation of the plate axleguard is available from MJT Components. Unfortunately, they are a tad oversize for many wagons. Furthermore, they are too deep to fit the OBA and OCA underframe. To ensure they fit, snip away the lugs as shown. It is unlikely to be easy to make this a compensated wagon.

7. Place the assembled axleguards in the wagon and mark in the position on the floor using a scalpel blade. The area between the lines will be cut away to reveal the underside of the wagon body, buying some much needed room!

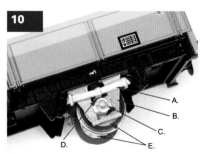

8. A network of holes drilled in the underframe makes this a quick task to complete.

9. The axleguard now rests on the underside of the wagon body, ensuring that the model rides at the correct height from the rail. Some 20thou styrene, which is just visible in this picture, is used as packing material to achieve the correct height.

10. The job is completed by adding cast spring (A) and axlebox (C) detail to each axleguard (B).

Additional detailing includes the fitting of brake discs to the wheels (E). Note that there is a gap between the axlebox and spring (D) which is difficult to avoid. It is helpful if compensation has been used.

11. The NEM coupling pocket and the bracket is cut off the axleguard assembly and glued directly to the underframe.
12. This picture shows the use of a No.18

Kadee coupling. All that remains is to fit a simple representation of the brake calipers.
13. The completed conversion, resulting in a rigid underframe, with enough room for compensated

axleguards, if those from the specialist societies are used (MJT Components ones are too large). The simple representation of brake calipers can be made out behind the axleguards.

14. The application of worn wood colour to the interior, rust to the inside surfaces of the body and other weathering effects helps to overcome the unsightly chunky wagon sides. The joints between the various drop down doors and the stanchions could be marked in with a scribing tool and

coloured with rust colours.
15. A slightly less battered Railfreight version is shown in this picture. The original livery is retained to save time, with weathering colours applied to the interior and dusted over the body, with an emphasis on rust shades.

Working with the vans

Although the axleguard arrangement fitted to the vans is the same as the open wagons, the body to underframe retaining screws are located close to the axleguard pivot spigot. Cutting the spigot away and either fitting new axleguards, as demonstrated with the OCA, or gluing the original plastic ones in place will make access to the screw holes impossible. If gluing the original axleguards in place, trim the centre section to reveal the screw holes so the body can be removed for weathering and other work. Alternatively, consider the sprung axleguards described later in the chapter, which could be screwed in place using the retaining screw that held the plastic axleguard in place. The following photographs show the work undertaken to the Bachmann VAA, including removal of the moulded ventilator from the Railfreight version.

1. Bachmann has chosen to provide the more unusual ventilated version of the VAA van in addition to the standard version. There were only 20 of these vehicles constructed to diagram 1/267 in 1969.
2. This picture of the end of the VAA shows the unusual ventilator and prominent ribs. For my

requirements, the ventilator was removed and the ribs smoothed down so they could barely be seen.

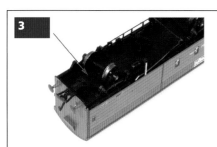

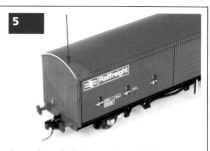

3. Underframe detail on the VAA/VBA van is fairly basic and there are a couple of minor errors including an error in the brake push rods on one side of the underframe. The axleguards are designed to be articulated to assist

operation on sharp curves.
4. The end ventilator is moulded as part of the body and is a solid piece of plastic to remove. Slow paring of the ventilator soon leaves a flat surface. Care should be taken not to damage

the roof lip which is something I did during this project. It had to be restored with some styrene strip.
5. The red arrow shows the remedial work to restore the roof line lip.

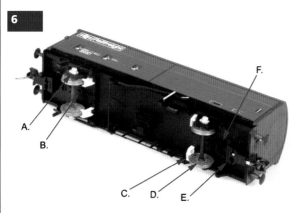

6. The body of both the VAA and VBA are not secured to the underframe with screws behind the headstocks, but through a hole under each axleguard assembly. This makes the fitting of the MJT Components and others' etched axleguards difficult to do without having to re-engineer the body fixings! The method used to initially get the wagon into service was to fix the articulated axle guards firmly in place so they did not rotate.
This picture shows the completed modification work:
A: Replacement axleboxes by S Kits
B: The plastic axleguard assemblies are fixed in place with a spot of glue so the screws are no longer needed
C: Simple representations of brake calliper brackets are fashioned from

'I'-section plastic strip
D: Etched disc brake inserts are fitted to the wheels. The wheels shown in this picture are by Ultrascale
E: The coupling bracket is relocated and fixed to the wagon floor so it does not move
F: The location of one of the two recesses which holds the body retaining screws. A notch is cut in both axleguard mouldings to allow access to them.
7. A weather strip composed of 10thou x 120thou styrene strip is applied across the top of the loading doors to represent the black rubberised strip applied to some full-size wagons.

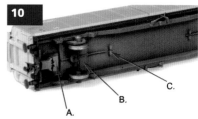

8. A thin wash of light grey paint dulls the original factory applied livery to a bleached appearance. Patch painting with Railfreight red over the bleached paint creates the appearance of a distressed paint job. The end ventilators are consigned to history, the marks finished off, overpainted. and together with weathering of

the roof, completes the picture.
9. The Bachmann VGA wagon is easier to work on – few modifications have been made to them and weathering can be easily achieved with washes of thinned roof dirt paint and underframe grime.
10. This model suffers from the same articulated axleguards as the Railfreight VAA

and VBA models. In this case, the coupling fixings are separated from the axleguards and glued permanently to the wagon floor (A). The axleguards are glued to the underframe (B) to improve performance. Note that the basic centre-return spring composed of a strip of plastic (C) is no longer needed.

Sprung suspension

Finescale modellers, particularly those working in P4 and S4 frequently extol the virtues of sprung compensation. If you have time available and do not mind fiddly modelling work, setting up springing for the longer wheelbase wagons, such as those described in this chapter does bring benefits in smoother running and good performance. Bill Bedford Models offers a variety of springing kits for ready-to-run and kit-built models, including sprung coach bogie frames and axleguards for fixed wheelbase wagons. In the range are axleguards for modern air-braked wagons which are ideal for the Railfreight vans, opens and sliding door vans offered by Bachmann. The Hornby OAA can also be enhanced with them and the improvement in running makes the work worthwhile.

Surprisingly, when you watch a completed sprung wagon model in action, you cannot see the axlebox assemblies moving up and down as you might observe on a real OCA or OBA as it crosses rail joints. Yet, the way in which the wagon rides is different. To make it work, the axlebox cover has to be separate from the springs and free to move up and down the slot in the axleguard. Care should also be taken at the painting stage to prevent paint from bonding the moving parts to the fixed axleguard.

A Bachmann OBA was used to test this method of suspension as the photographs show. The original axleguards were removed completely and the coupling mounts separated so they could be fixed to the wagon floor in very much the same manner as the other wagons described in this chapter. The screw fixing spigots on the floor of the wagon were retained because the etched axleguards supplied by Bill Bedford Models have a hole in the middle which enables the folded axleguard assembly to fit over the spigot. This ensures the axleguard fits perfectly and is correctly positioned on the centre line of the wagon. The moving part of each axleguard is fitted with a length of springy steel wire which acts as the suspension spring, fitted to the axleguard by threading the ends of the wire into their mounts. The axlebox is fitted to the exterior face and a bearing fitted on the inside. Clip in a wheelset to test and adjust as necessary.

With both axleguard assemblies and wheels in place, the model can be adjusted for ride height (my test example came out at almost the exact height) and when satisfied that the wheels do not slop about in the axleguards, preventing the spring part from doing its work, do a test run on the layout. Painting runs the risk of seizing things up, so apply paint with an airbrush rather than a paint brush and mist it in place a thin layer at a time. Applying a spot of model oil along the moving parts before painting will do much to prevent the paint from gumming up the works!

Sprung suspension fitted to a Bachmann OBA. Very little modification to the wagon underframe was necessary other than the relocation of the coupling fixings and discarding the original plastic axleguards. The Bill Bedford Models sprung axleguards fitted perfectly!

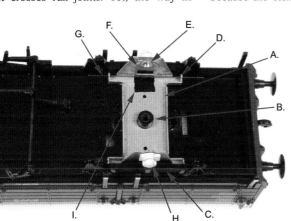

A closer look at the work done to the OBA

A: The fixed axleguard composed of etched-brass and folded before installation
B: The original screw spigot is retained as the axleguard fits over it perfectly
C: The moulded cosmetic suspension detail is retained
D: Extensions to the axleguard hold the ends of the wire that provides the suspension effect
E: 2mm diameter waisted bearings are used in this system
F: The moving part of the axleguard assembly which slides up and down a slot in the fixed part
G: Springing wire
H: Cosmetic axlebox cover fitted to the moving part
I: The slot behind the axleguards is opened up so that the wheel flange of OO and EM wheels will not touch it

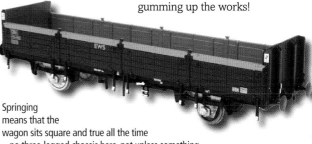

Springing means that the wagon sits square and true all the time – no three-legged chassis here, not unless something horribly wrong with the conversion has happened. Note that there is a slight gap between the axlebox cover and cosmetic suspension springs which allows for the movement necessary to make this system work effectively.

ABOVE: VBA No.200017 was photographed at Didcot in faded Railfreight livery in June 2003. The original Railfreight markings have been painted over and the resulting patch is in a slightly brighter shade of Railfreight red than the rest of the livery.

LEFT: VAA and VBA vans found in the yard at Didcot are usually used on Ministry of Defence traffic and can be adorned with a variety of Hazchem notices. However, VAA No.200126 show signs of various notices having been scraped off the door over the years and the livery itself is faded and patched.

BELOW: VGA No.210465 was caught on camera at Didcot when in use on MoD traffic. Note the Carlisle Currock wagon works emblem, which takes the form of a stylised fox, and traces of hazardous materials notices. These wagons work between locations such as Bicester, Didcot and the military port at Marchwood.

ABOVE: There is more evidence of weathering on VGA No. 210484 than the van in the previous photograph. The yellow ends of this Railfreight Distribution liveried van have faded and show signs of rusting.

RIGHT: Battered, rusting but still in traffic: OCA No. 112177 has one painted panel in EWS maroon with the data panel painted on it. The rusting scrapes and marks can easily be represented with quick drying oil paint and careful streaking with turps.

BELOW: An OCA painted in former engineers' yellow/grey livery shows rusting scrapes in the paint and streaking where the rain has washed rust staining down the paint. This wagon is No.112394, which was in good running order otherwise, despite its outwardly distressed appearance which, when applied to the Bachmann OCA model, adds much character.

OCA No.112390 was photographed at Toton on July 9, 2004 when in EWS ownership. The original Railfreight markings have been painted out and the wagon is adorned with post-1998 electrification warning flashes. A detail consistent with the Bachmann model is that the axleboxes are painted maroon.

LEFT: The livery on OCA No.112200 is a mixture of EWS maroon and rust. This wagon was one of the few to be painted in EWS colours with a small logo on the centre doors.

BELOW: The bodies of OBAs are constructed of wood which has been replaced many times over the years. OBA No.110457 is in pretty good condition, painted EWS maroon externally and with unpainted wood on the interior which has weathered to a silvery grey and brown colour. That unpainted wood colour is not easy to represent with paints and is best done by painting the planks a light grey, washing a darker grey with traces of brown over it, to give depth and variety to the colours.

ABOVE: Fresh repairs are evident on OBA No.110053. Note the unpainted and unweathered wood on the drop door nearest the camera. Other doors appear to have been repaired, with new planks and the strapping appears to be new too. As a note of interest, during 2008 some OBAs were being fitted with mesh doors as part of an overhaul at Warrington to equip them for block traffic.

RIGHT: Headstock and buffer detail of OBA No.110472.

LEFT: Parabolic spring detail (known as Bruninghaus) of OBA No.110472 shows how the wagon sits when empty. This picture gives an idea as to why the Bill Bedford Models sprung axleguard system is both authentic and practical.

LEFT: Many of the former Railfreight air braked open goods wagons find work as material recovery wagons. These are filled with all sorts of material recovered from a work site, including some unused new materials left over from the job.

BELOW: OTA No. 210144 is a former VDA van modified for timber traffic. The bases for the timber stanchions are different to those on OTA No. 210170 below. The van retains its Transrail grey livery. Note the steel floor and ratchet tensioners which can be obtained as a detailing component. It is possible to model this wagon using the Bachmann VDA van model, cutting down the body and adding new details with brass section and detailing components.

The origins of this former VDA van are still apparent. The ends were retained even though the roof and doors have been removed to convert it to timber traffic. New stanchions are fitted to new pockets welded to the sides, a detail that varies depending on when the conversion was undertaken. In this case, this is one done for EWS, whilst others are older. Many of these conversions were not repainted, resulting in colourful trains. The TOPS data panel is applied to the wagon ends which shows the original VDA running number 210170.

ABOVE: A redundant OBA was shorn of its body to create a useful runner vehicle or RRA. The underframe is unchanged, including the floor of the wagon. The doors and ends are gone, as have the door bangers. Only the bolt holes remain! This represents an interesting variation that can be simply modelled by removing the sides and ends from the Bachmann model.

RIGHT: OTA No.112264 was rebuilt from a redundant OCA including new ends and stanchion fittings.

BELOW: Many ballast and spoil wagons were constructed from redundant van underframes. ZCA No.DC200296 was once a former VBA van. When photographed in April 2008, it retained yellow/grey livery and the prefix DC.

Unique liveried Class 66, No.66 066 passes Burton-on-Trent with a north bound steel train comprising of a mix of BAA and BBA steel carrying wagons loaded with slabs of steel. Whilst a model of 60 066 has been offered by Hornby, no manufacturer has, to date, taken advantage of the use of parts common to the various members of the BAA and BBA wagon family such as the FTB6 bogie. However, this could change!

So far, this book has presented a run down of techniques and ideas to get you going at detailing and improving wagon models in your collection. This chapter looks at a cross-section of some popular models which do not fit any of the previous chapters. This includes some new (as of 2008) models such as the Hornby 'Rudd', 'Clam' and 'Tope' ballast wagons which were hot off the production line at the time of writing. No book can keep up with developments and as this one was in planning, Bachmann announced their JJA auto-ballaster wagons, Dapol was putting the finishing touches to its FEA-B, telescopic hood wagon and a 'Grampus', whilst Heljan was showing off images of its IGA Cargowaggon flat wagon. None of these will meet the print deadline!

Hornby ZCV and ZBA wagons

Hornby continued to develop its range of engineers' wagons in 2008, adding a 'Shark' ballast plough brake van to the range early in the year. Also anticipated by modellers were three new models of popular engineers' wagons from the BR Sectorisation era which are based on one standard underframe and are rebuilds of former HTV coal hoppers. The ZCV 'Tope,' with its complex hopper shape, is a cut-down 21t HTV coal hopper which was used in large numbers, until they were replaced by air-braked wagons with more robust bodies. Its box-body cousin, the ZCV 'Clam' has a more robust body, with numerous vertical ribs, which makes painting in yellow/grey engineers livery quite challenging. Finally, and by far the longest surviving of the three, is the ZBA 'Rudd', an air-braked rebuild using the former HTV underframe. All of them date from the later 1980s and early 1990s.

As you can imagine, these wagons did not remain pristine for very long and the vacuum brakes fitted to the 'Tope' and 'Clam' were a distinct hindrance, ensuring their swift withdrawal from grace (and traffic) in the post-privatisation era. As newer air braked wagons such as the MHA (built on former HAA underframes) and cut-down MEAs made their way into ballast and spoil duties, the 'Rudd', despite its air-brakes, became an increasingly rare wagon too.

The Hornby models are pristine, making them suitable subjects for all kinds of weathering, rusting and battering, these techniques are described in the next chapter. The bodies are just begging for a battering to make them less like exhibition models and more like something exposed to the merciless action of mechanical grabs when out at weekends, or during unloading at spoil tips during the week. That does depend when you are modelling them; when introduced, they were pretty pristine, having been fully repainted, even if the paint finishes became quickly sun-bleached to a pale grey and even paler yellow. Renumbering transfers for 'Rudds' are currently available from Scale Model Transfers by Frank Design (www.scalemodeltransfers.co.uk).

Shunting locomotives often get in on the act on the main line with short transfer freights such as this photograph of grey Class 09, No. 09 203 passing through Newport with a mix of covered steel wagons including a JSA (Andersley and S-kits) and a BYA (Bachmann).

Hornby's air braked ZBA 'Rudd' dressed in engineers' yellow and grey livery.

The ZCV 'Clam' with its heavily ribbed box body and beautifully applied paint finish.

The Hornby models are pristine, making them suitable subjects for all kinds of weathering, rusting and battering. Unfortunately, the models featured here were pre-production models and had to be returned to Hornby in the pristine condition in which they are seen here. Rust coloured paint, thinners, micro brushes, cocktail sticks and other such tools of the weathering trade remained in the paint box!

Of the three wagons in this batch, the ZCV 'Tope' is by far the most impressive, with fine handrails and many small details apparent on the body. Note the position of the vacuum cylinder.

The underframe offered by Hornby is correctly fitted with roller bearing axle boxes and the models come fitted with correct three-hole disc wheels. Small details, including the brake gear, are assembled from standalone parts.

LEFT: Hornby has equipped the models with a sprung close-coupling cam mechanism which has a NEM coupling pocket. This accepts Kadee No.18 couplers (as seen in this photograph) with ease and is fitted to the correct height.

ABOVE: ZCV ('Tope') No. DB 970010 was photographed at Didcot in June 1997, bringing up the rear of a train of similar wagons. Its external condition is poor and much of the original livery has been taken over by rust. Note that the lower part of the hopper can be seen below the underframe.

CENTRE RIGHT: 'Tope' No. DB 970639 was condemned when this picture was taken. It varies from the earlier picture of DB 970010 in that there is no lower part of the hopper to be seen as represented by the Hornby model. The livery is nearly original except for the Transrail logo.

RIGHT: The heavily ribbed box body of a ZCV 'Clam' is unmistakable. Note the use of three-hole disc wheels and spindle buffers which are left over from the underframe's days as a coal hopper wagon. The running number has been applied to the solebar and reads DB 973255.

ZCV No. 973086 takes part in engineering work in May 1997.

Table 1: Rudd, Clam and Tope number sequences

Wagon type:	Date converted:	Number sequence:
ZCV 'Tope'	1987-88	DB970000-970059 with gaps
ZCV 'Tope'	1989-91	DB970100-970855
ZBA 'Rudd'	1989-91	DB972000-972799
ZCV 'Clam'	1989-90	DB973000-973449

The underframe offered by Hornby is correctly fitted with roller bearing axleboxes and the model comes fitted with correct three-hole disc wheels. Interestingly, there is sufficient room between the axleguards to accept P4 and EM wheels. Plenty of room in fact, and Hornby has fitted axles of 27mm in length to suit the wagon. This is awkward for wheel-changers like me and the solution is to re-use the supplied axles by swapping the wheels over.

Hornby has equipped the models with a sprung close-coupling cam mechanism which has a NEM coupling pocket. This accepts Kadee No.18 couplers with ease and is fitted at the correct height. When the wagons are fitted with the shortest of the NEM Kadee couplings, the No.17, quite close coupling can be achieved. The underframes are equipped with many fine details, including in-line brake blocks, individual brake details (except the 'Tope' which correctly has the vacuum cylinder located on an end platform) and turned metal buffers. Overall, they look the part, unimpressive, ordinary and everyday wagons ready for a tough life in the engineers' fleet. As models though, they are impressive!

Hornby 'Shark'

Hornby released three versions of the ZUV ballast plough brake van in early 2008 and they sold like mad, especially the 'Dutch' liveried example. The model is based on Diagram 1/597 with planked body, square oil axleboxes and vacuum brakes. The model features self-contained buffers and a tall vacuum pipe and represents the wagon in 'as built' condition, without any of the modifications, repairs and additions applied to the vans during their working lives. Attempts to update the full-size vans has included replacing the planking with plywood and, in some cases, steel sheet together with updating the running gear with air brakes. Hornby's position on this is understandable because to introduce even one variation on the theme would make the model specific to one vehicle only, given that the majority of upgrades and repairs made each van virtually unique.

The (nice) problem with the Hornby 'Shark' is that it looks far too pristine when compared to the tatty, dilapidated and decaying examples that could be

Hornby could not possibly do a better job of the model than they have, especially given its retail price of £14.50 at the time of release. A large number of stand-alone parts have been used to enhance the appearance of the model. One small detail to note: the body is fitted to the chassis the wrong way round. The stove chimney should be on the same side as the underframe 'vee' hanger

The underframe represents a wagon to diagram 1/597 with vacuum brakes. Some additional details are required to model an air-braked example as represented by the livery applied to this version of the model. Hornby provide additional, full-size ploughs for those wishing to dispense with the slotted ploughs and tension lock couplings.

found around the rail network, especially in the last ten years. Despite this, you cannot disguise the fact that these vehicles are very difficult to spruce up, unless in model form! This offers an opportunity to weather and distress the model to your heart's content, if that is your thing.

Hornby could not possibly do a better job of the model than they have. A large number of stand-alone parts, such as separate handrails, add to its fine appearance. The model comes with a small bag of additional detailing parts, including alternative ploughs, to suit those modellers who wish to fit scale couplings.

Upon taking the model from the box, one is immediately struck by its weight, which is nearly 100g in total. Despite all that fine detail, it has a good solid feel to it, with parts securely fixed in place. Here is a run down of the individual features on this model, as many of them are noteworthy in making this the best ready-to-run wagon in the Hornby range.

The vacuum brake cylinder, push rods and vee hangers are nicely executed using stand-alone parts. Brake blocks line up with the wheels and include the yokes, which means that it would not take too much time to add the additional linkages to accurately model the brakes. Modellers of the up-

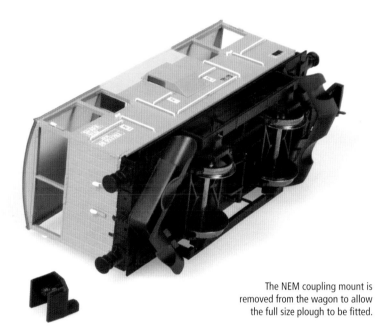

The NEM coupling mount is removed from the wagon to allow the full size plough to be fitted.

to-date scene may wish to modify the underframe with S-Kits cast metal detailing parts to represent the air-braked version.

NEM coupling pockets are fitted to the underframe and appear to be at the specified height for use with Kadee No.17 or 18 couplers, depending on how close the coupling is required to be. The ploughs fitted to the van as supplied have a gap to clear the coupling, resulting in a very neat appearance. A set of full ploughs is included in the box for those modellers who wish to dispose of the

tension lock couplings and fit screw couplings instead.

The Hornby bodyshell is a lot neater than that found on the real thing! It features flush-glazed cabin windows, some very fine detailing for the plough mechanism and a number of small separately applied lamp irons (correctly off-set on each end). The body and roof are separate mouldings, attached to the underframe with two screws. A large ballast weight occupies almost all of the space below the window-line within the cabin, although it is hidden

Not a typical 'Shark,' but one that has seen much repair to the body, with plywood extensively used. ZUV No. DB 993746 is the wagon in question, painted in Mainline Freight blue and photographed at Didcot in October 1997. It was originally built in 1956 by the Birmingham RC&W Co.

from view. This has left the verandah clear so it may be detailed with a figure or two.

So, what a perfect little model upon

which to base some interesting conversions. If one is prepared to do some patch-painting or full repainting, the planks could be filled with a putty-

type filler to represent a van patched and repaired with plywood. Distressed effects can be introduced by chiselling gently into the bodyshell, the model as supplied has little wood grain in the planking. On the full-sized vans, even those recently painted, it is possible to see wood grain striking through the paint. Some gentle work with a fibreglass pencil is an alternative way of creating this wood grain effect.

The roof as supplied is immaculate, but in reality the roofing felt became torn, patched and otherwise less than perfect. There are numerous techniques to represent the effect of distressed roofing material. Another challenge would be to try and represent those planks that have slipped very slightly in relation to their neighbours. In addition, rusting effects could be applied to the ploughs, together with ballast dust and brake dusting to the underframe. In short, you could spend rather a lot of time beating up this model.

A close match to the Hornby model is 'Shark' No. DB 993753, photographed at Didcot in July 1997. It was still wearing very faded engineers yellow/grey livery at the time and appeared to be fairly intact – no plywood to be seen, at least not on this side of the vehicle. Note the tall vacuum pipe on the end. This too was constructed in 1956 by the Birmingham RC&W Co.

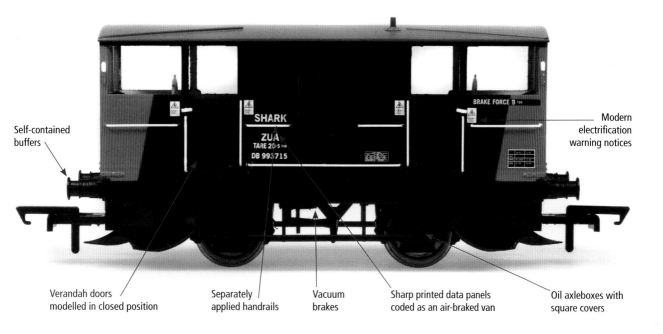

Self-contained buffers

Modern electrification warning notices

SHARK
ZUA
TARE 20·5 ㎜
DB 993715

BRAKE FORCE 9 ㎜

Verandah doors modelled in closed position

Separately applied handrails

Vacuum brakes

Sharp printed data panels coded as an air-braked van

Oil axleboxes with square covers

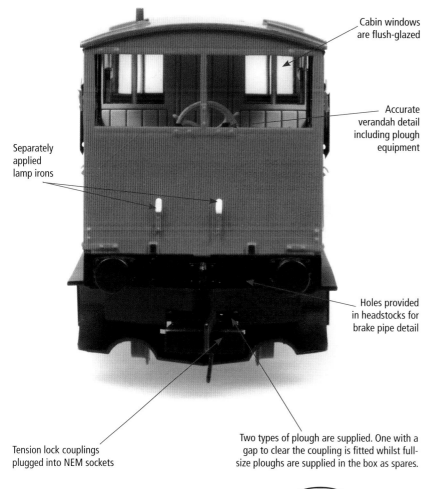

Cabin windows are flush-glazed

Accurate verandah detail including plough equipment

Separately applied lamp irons

Holes provided in headstocks for brake pipe detail

Tension lock couplings plugged into NEM sockets

Two types of plough are supplied. One with a gap to clear the coupling is fitted whilst full-size ploughs are supplied in the box as spares.

Hornby china clay CDA

Mainstay of the china clay circuits in Cornwall is the CDA hopper, an adaptation of the successful MGR wagon used on power station coal circuits. A total of 123 wagons were built at Doncaster in 1987 and 1988, with an additional 14 converted from MGR wagons in 1989. Numbered 375000 – 375137, some wagons are used for specific types of clay and are marked accordingly.

Hornby has adapted its new version of the HAA MGR wagon with a moulded top to represent the cover and roll-top bar, together with the required mechanism. It's a fair effort which has been carried out without retooling the wagon itself. Noting that these wagons are 'handed', there is no representation of the slots found on one side (the same side as the platform mounted brake distributor) and the fitting of the moulded top itself is not exactly like the full-size CDA. Strangely enough, the buffers are correct for this type of wagon, but not a coal HAA, as discussed earlier in the book. Many of the techniques for improving the running of wheels and bearings, together with other details are

Hornby has dressed its CDA hopper in weathered EWS livery for the 2008 catalogue. Modellers familiar with china clay traffic will know that these wagons become very dusty indeed.

The moulded top is a low-cost compromise to convert the Hornby HAA model into a CDA. It works to a certain extent and could be further improved with detailing. The brake distributor detail and buffers are correct for this type of wagon.

described in the chapter on bulk coal wagons. CDAs were the ideal companion to Class 37s, particularly the St. Blazey fleet of freight Class 37/5 locomotives in the 37 6xx number sequence and a handful of 37/4s too. Class 66 locomotives are used on those freight circuits today.

The Bachmann BRA and BYA

The EWS BYA and BRA covered steel carrying wagons can be found all over the country, singly, in pairs, or in short rakes. This means that modellers can mix them in with other wagons in mixed rakes, or run them singly if desired with most EWS motive power. Precision manufacturing such as that found in the automotive and similar industries demand high quality semi-finished steel to ensure consistent quality and durability of the final product. Key to the process and often regarded as an integral part of the manufacturing process is the distribution phase and damage to steel such as coil can be costly and disruptive.

The new wagons were constructed by Thrall Europa at York, to one basic design that could be adapted for the transportation of either coil or rod. The majority of the 310 wagons were fitted for coils, with features designed to protect the coils including hardwood lining to prevent steel to steel contact, sealed troughs to prevent contamination and covers to keep the rain out. The covers are lightweight and corrugated for strength, giving the wagon a distinctive appearance similar to Nissen huts. Each of the three covers slide along the length of the wagon and are telescopic. Thus the wagon does not have a line of symmetry across its width; the bulkhead at one end is

Table 2: Leading dimensions of the Bachmann BRA and BYA wagons

	Prototype dimensions	Scale dimensions	Model dimensions
Length over buffers	14,618mm	191.7mm	192.0mm
Length over couplings	14,796mm	194.0mm	197.0mm
Length over headstocks	13,378mm	175.5mm	176.0mm
Width	27,56mm	36.0mm	36.0mm
Height from rail	37,72mm	49.5mm	49.0mm
Bogie centres	95,80mm	125.5mm	125.5mm
Bogie centre to headstocks	18,99mm	25.0mm	25.0mm
Bogie wheelbase	1,829mm	24.0mm	24.0mm
Buffer length	620mm	8.0mm	7.5mm
Coupler mid-point from rail	964mm	12.5mm	12.0mm

Table 3: TOPS running number details as built

TOPS Code	Design Code	Numbers
Steel coil wagon - BYA	BY006	966001 – 260.
Strip steel wagon - BRA	BR008A/B	964001 – 050.

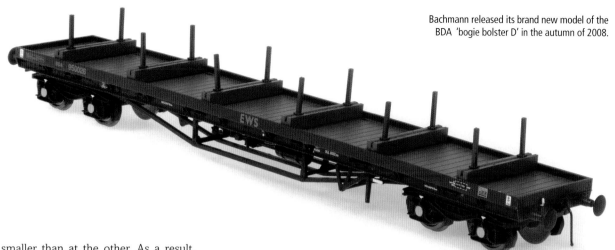

smaller than at the other. As a result, the complete length of the wagon can be made accessible for loading without having to remove the covers. Notably, the lightweight design makes them prone to accidental damage when loading. In recent years, many of the original covers have been replaced completely with light red (unpainted) new ones.

Turning our attention to the Bachmann model, the Nissen hut appearance with ribbing and crinkles in the covers is quite well captured, as is

the overall curved profile. The ends of the wagon are fitted with hood locking equipment and the knuckle coupling release lever, which are all individually fitted small details. The headstocks have a representation of the coupling hook, nicely moulded square buffers and a hole to fit a single air-brake pipe.

The use of individually fitted parts is also apparent on the underframe, with handbrake wheels, footsteps and pipe runs being all well-defined mouldings.

Each wagon rides on nicely tooled representations of Thrall National Swing Motion bogies of 6' wheelbase (approximately). Brake blocks are in-line with the wheels and the sideframes are spaced at 23mm between the inside faces, so there is sufficient room to fit EM and P4 wheels. The axleboxes do not have the end detail as on the prototype.

The wheels supplied with the model

The Bachmann BYA/BRA wagon is highly regarded and rightly so. The Nissen hut appearance with ribbing and crinkles in the covers is quite well captured, as is the overall curved profile. The ends of the wagon are fitted with hood locking equipment and the knuckle coupling release lever, all individually fitted small details. This model has been lightly weathered and patched before being placed into use.

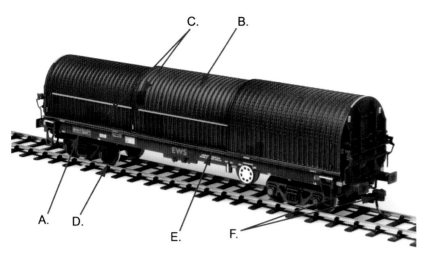

When good models like this are available, more attention can be placed on weathering and the small details. This BYA has been renumbered with transfers from Fox Transfers (A), weathered with a sun bleaching effect (B), patch painted over the bleaching to show areas of repair to the hoods (C) and rusted in areas which wear or are unpainted, such as the runners (E), wheel faces (D) buffers and couplings (F).

Transfers for data panels ands number sets are available from Fox Transfers for renumbering the wagons from the box. The colour match is excellent and the job takes a few minutes.

Arrow (A) points to the scale height coupling box which is fitted with an EZMate coupling when the model is taken from the box. You can also use the NEM coupler pocket sockets to use the supplied tension lock coupling or fit a Kadee No.18 or 19 coupling. When the NEM coupling pocket adapter is fitted (B), Kadee couplers are a simple plug-in fitting.

are metal, with 'blackening' that appears a dark brown colour, not dissimilar to the colour of the wheels on the wagons when delivered new from York. I discovered that my Ultrascale 12mm diameter disc wheels fitted this model without difficulty. A very small amount of material was shaved from the surface of each brake shoe to ensure that the wheels were free running.

Much comment was made about the seemingly arbitrary fitting height of the EZMate couplings supplied with the model. The centre-line of the coupling is 12mm from the rail, approximately 3mm greater than the operational height of Kadee couplings. Examination of works drawings shows the knuckle coupling at a height of 964mm on to the prototype, which equates to 12.5mm (to the nearest half millimetre). So the model is scale in this respect, if operationally irritating from a modeller's viewpoint.

The bogies are fitted with NEM coupler pocket sockets and so conversion to either tension lock or Kadee No.18 and 19 couplings is possible without too much trouble. When the NEM coupling pocket adapter is fitted, Kadee couplers are a simple plug-in fitting.

Overall, the model is lightweight, weighing in at an average of 84 grammes. Additional weight could be concealed in the body with ease.

Heljan ferry van

Operated on the prototype railways as single wagons within mixed freight trains and in long rakes of similar wagons, the new Heljan Cargowaggon should find a home on layouts both large and small. As models go, it is pretty large, at nearly 290mm in length some owners of small layouts will need to carefully consider the impact that such a large wagon will have on their operations.

Of all freight wagon models, vans are amongst the most useful vehicles that can be used on a model railway because, unless the doors are modelled in the open position on a static model, there are none of the issues of modelling a

Table 4: Scale dimensions for a Habfis 2 Cargowaggon:

	Prototype dimension (mm)	Scale dimension (mm)	Dimension on model (mm)	Variance (+/-) (mm)
Length over buffers	21,700	285	284	-1
Length over end panels	20,440	268	268	0
Bogie wheelbase	1,800	23.6	22.9	-0.7
Bogie centres	16,660	218.5	219	+0.5
Overall height from rail	3,946	51.5	51.2	negligible
Length of loading doors	10,069	132	132	0
Height of floor from rail	1,230	16.2	16	negligible
Width over panels	2,600	34	33.25	-0.75
Wheel diameter	920	12	11.8	-0.2

loaded or empty box or flat wagon. Another benefit of operating large vans is that they can be used to represent almost any traffic including steel, commodities such as glass, foodstuffs, wine and packaging materials, bagged products such as cement, fertiliser and china clay together with finished industrial components such as automotive parts. In reality, the list of traffics that common vans such as the Heljan Cargowaggon are employed are endless.

Heljan offered its first batch of Cargowaggons in 2007, with eight different liveries; including those with

It's good to see a version of a model in a nondescript livery which could be personalised with specific weathering and then 'lost' amongst other wagons on the layout as another ordinary run-of-the-mill ferry van. It is important to have as much of the 'routine' as possible to create realistic scenes on a layout and this model fits the bill perfectly.

A 'Cargowaggon' liveried model poses on the author's layout. It looks the part, although weathering would tone down the shiny finish very nicely indeed. This model will be very popular due to its versatility in a variety of different traffics.

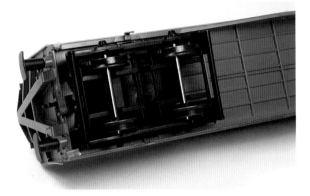

Although equipped with NEM coupling pockets, they are not fitted to the published specification and as this image shows, they are too high.

ABOVE LEFT: The bogie mouldings are basic to say the least, even though they are equipped with separate brake block details. It is challenging to fit closer-to-scale wheels to this model and the use of a slippery tough black plastic will make work on the bogies 'interesting'.

ABOVE RIGHT: The bogie pivots are basic too; no attempt has been done to incorporate any form of compensation about the bogie pivot. The models 'wobble' when operated on a layout.

BELOW: It is tempting to model the GERS-registered KFA wagons (GERS 97xxx-series) using the Heljan model. Note that the end detail of timber KFAs is different to the Heljan model. There is no reason why the end detail cannot be changed using plastic strip. Any difference in the length of the full-size KFA compated to the model is also a consideration when looking at this as a possible conversion.

markings representing ownership after the acquisition of Cargowaggon by GE Rail Services, Cargowaggon livery and a plain silver and blue livery which can be weathered until the wagon looks like any other nondescript van sitting in a yard. The model appears very impressive indeed due to its physical presence. It has much to commend it, being of an accurate shape with crisp and finely executed tooling. In terms of its overall appearance, the model looks exactly like the prototype. Features include some separate handrails (some are moulded), NEM coupling pockets fitted to a close coupling mechanism concealed within the body and a fine representation of the large buffers, which all add character to this model. There are also some applied details, including ferry securing hooks, brake wheels and buffers.

The body is separately moulded from the floor and underframe and is equipped with a separate roof panel. It is accurately moulded, with the correct spacing and moulded grab rails at the end of each loading door. Bodyside loading doors are well executed and capture the plain, angular character of these large vehicles very well. Unfortunately, there is no sign

Hornby offers a basic but useful model for the PG013E PGA aggregate wagon.

of individually applied components for brake rodding, brake gear, air tanks and air cylinders on the underframe.

When attempting to fit closer-to-scale wheels on this model, I discovered that a normal 4mm scale wheelset with RP25/88 wheels and 26mm length axles would not fit as a drop-in replacement – the bogies were distorted by the longer axle. Thus, EM and P4 modellers will encounter some difficulty when changing the wheels, because there is a mere 22.3mm between the inside faces of the bogie frames.

The bogie frames are 29.6mm apart over the external axleboxes, which means that it should be

possible to modify the bogies to accept wheelsets with 26mm length axles. I found that drilling out the axleboxes (carefully) and installing plain 2mm bearings, shortened with a file, meant I could convert the model to EM gauge using my 'stock' wheelsets. It is possible to obtain EM wheels with shorter axles that should fit, but this will be of no help to P4 modellers!

NEM coupling pockets are supplied, together with a sprung, close coupling mechanism which is concealed in the body of the wagon. No more than a casual glance at the tension lock couplings supplied with the model reveals that there is a slight step between the fish-tail fitting and the coupling itself. Testing the model with a Kadee No.19 coupler and height gauge revealed that the NEM box is mounted higher than the published standard.

Hornby PGA

Modelled on the Procor constructed PGAs of 1980, the model is reasonably accurate to Diagram PG013E (PR14333-14388). It has the correct shape of hopper and the underframe is equipped with the correct Gloucester suspension. There is little doubt that the age of the tooling is apparent, with many coarse features begging to be refined by some careful modelling and the use of etched and cast components. As a base model,

The same model is seen dressed in ECC Quarries livery.

Although the detail on the model shows its age, there is much that can be done with it to detail it with cast and etched components from S-Kits and A1 Models.

A: Replace the chunky end platforms **B:** Paint and weather the interior of the hopper **C:** Remove moulding lines from the headstocks **D:** Remove mould lines from the buffers or replace them completely **E:** Fit etched brass ladders **F:** Replace the brake wheels **G:** Replace the moulded brake detail with castings.

it is ideal for detailing and some conversion projects too, including the earlier PG013C type with BSC Friction suspension, BIS sand hoppers (add the roof hatches) and other similar PAA covered hoppers.

Moulded detail that can easily be replaced with quality after-market components include the buffers, air tanks, brake wheels, air distributor, end platforms and ladders. Cast metal representations of the Gloucester suspension units could also be fitted if so desired.

This makes a classic super detail project which is easy to complete and could be undertaken whilst retaining the well-applied livery and simply patch painting new details with the appropriate colour. Weathering would soon blend everything together in terms of overall appearance.

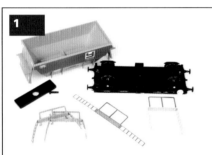

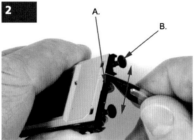

1. The model is dismantled by releasing the screw in the underframe. The new etched end platforms and ladder assemblies are also shown.

2. Much of this project involves removing the traces of coarse tooling such as the coupling hook (A) and moulding lines from the buffer

faces (B) and the headstocks. Scrape them away carefully with a modelling knife.
3. Clean up with fine wet and dry paper.

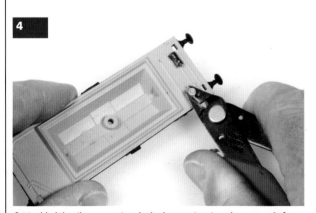

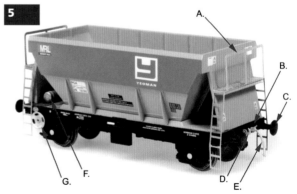

4. Moulded detail representing the brake gear is snipped away ready for better defined cast details.
5. The finished article ready for patch painting:
A: A1 Models etched end platform, ladder and handrail detail

B: Headstocks cleaned of moulding lines **C:** Buffers cleaned of moulding lines **D:** New cast coupling hooks fitted **E:** Air brake pipes by Shawplan Models **F:** New air receiving tank and other brake equipment details by S-Kits **G:** New cast brake wheels by S-Kits.

Bachmann 'Queen Mary' brake van

Bachmann offers a pretty good model of the 25t SR bogie brake van in a variety of liveries to Diagram 1550, as built at Ashford in 1936. The model is pretty accurate and represents a vacuum braked version with full planked sides and is supplied with end sandboxes when appropriate. The model is represented in 'as built' condition, without many of the modern refinements that we see on the few that survived into the diesel and electric era, such as airbrakes. Wooden bodied vehicles such as this also see numerous changes as they undergo repairs to the planking, so reference photographs are essential.

The base model for this project to model ADS 56299 was the grey coloured barrier vehicle intended for stone traffic (catalogue No.33.289) without the end sandboxes common to this type of van. My choice of EWS YTX was once offered by Bachmann with the same number (ADS 56299) and the same as the one featured in the photographs of the full-size van. The similarity ends at the livery, because

The Bachmann models are quite presentable and most diesel era modellers could justify one at a push. However, the model is as per the original SR Diagram 1550, with vacuum brakes. The end sandboxes are separate detailing items that are included by Bachmann depending on the prototype modelled. Some of the livery versions do not match the vacuum brake arrangement.

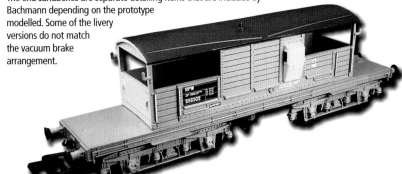

the real ADS 56299 has numerous detail differences, including the fitting of air brake equipment.

Careful examination of the model against the photographs taken at Walsall reveals a number of cosmetic detail differences:

- ADS 56299 is dual-braked. The underframe is equipped with an air cylinder, reservoir tank and distributor linked to the existing brake levers. The airbrake equipment can be observed from the side with the plated verandah door (for the sake of argument, identified as side A).
- The wagon retains two vacuum cylinders. These are relocated to one side of the wagon, that which has two planked verandah doors. (Side B).
- One verandah door is plated (on side A) whilst the rest of the van is planked.
- Roof rain strips are of a different pattern to the model and missing in parts, a feature that gives the model character when included.
- Roofing felt is secured along the edges of the roof with pieces of wood, missing in parts.
- The stovepipe is different in detail to the model.

Table 5: Model dimensions against prototype

	Prototype (actual)	Prototype (Scale)	Model
Length over buffers	40' 0"	160mm	160mm
Length over headstocks	36' 6"	146mm	146mm
Height from rail	11' 3¾"	45.2mm	44mm
Bogie wheelbase	8' 0"	32mm	32mm
Bogie centres	21' 0"	84mm	84mm
Width over footsteps or duckets	8' 0"	32mm	33mm
Width over cornice	7' 6"[1]	30mm	30mm

[1] Figure 43 in *An Illustrated History of Southern Wagons* – Vol. 4 has this dimension as 8' 4" whilst the drawing scales at 30mm or 7' 6"

Table 6: 25t bogie brake vans believed to be in service as of January 2002

Number	TOPS	Design code	Notes:
ADS 56284	YTV	YT500A	
ADS 56286	YTX	YT500C	EWS livery
ADS 56289	YTV	YT500A	Steel plating on cabin sides
DS 56296	YTX	YT500C	
ADS 56299	YTX	YT500C	EWS livery
ADS 56303	YTA	YT500E	Sandboxes retained. Painted in Railfreight sector colours
ADS 56304	YTV	YT500A	NSE blue with sandboxes
ADS 56305	YTW	YT500D	EWS livery

- Round 'Oleo' buffers have replaced the original type.
- Wagon label clips and other small details are located differently.

To complete the project, the following components and materials were used:
- 14mm coach disc wheels
- Air pipes (Shawplan)
- 'Oleo' buffers, air cylinder and reservoir tank (S-Kits)
- Express Models flashing tail lamp kit designed for DCC operation
- Styrene strip for rain strips and other roof parts
- Transfers from a variety of Fox Transfers' packs for EWS livery
- EWS colours from Phoenix Precision Paints

It is only after the model is broken down into its constituent parts that the modeller discovers how basic this model actually is. The ballast weight is too large and obstructs the space that otherwise could be used to add character, such as open verandah doors, staff, tail lamps, shunter's equipment and, of course, wooden

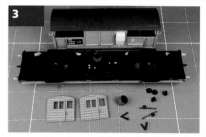

1. The bogies of the Bachmann 'Queen Mary' brake are nicely detailed and will accept EM gauge wheels at a pinch. However P4 wheels are impossible to get in without modifications.
2. A view of the vacuum brake cylinders and

'V'-hangers is offered in this photograph. The vacuum cylinders can be unplugged and relocated to the opposite side of the wagon to make room for the air brake equipment.
3. The model can be broken down into

manageable sub-assemblies for detailing and painting. One feature is the large ballast weight, which fills both the cabin and verandah areas, making the detailing of the verandahs difficult.

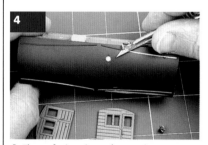
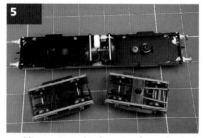

4. The roof rain strips and stove pipe are removed from the roof and replaced with slightly different variants made up from styrene strip and tube.
5. New detail is added to the underframe

moulding to create the character of a modernised wagon. Airbrake detail and other fittings are as important to establish the period for which the wagon is being modelled as the livery.
6. White styrene reveals the changes on this

unpainted model, including the plated verandah door and changes to the roof. A planked floor can just be seen through the part-open doors, a detail not possible to achieve unless the ballast weight is modified.

7. A flashing tail light was regarded as essential for this brake van. A kit was installed comprising of a circuit designed to rectify the track current normally used for DCC and a light store feature that keeps the light flashing should power be interrupted for a few seconds by factors such as dirty track. The wires from the current collection

wipers can be seen in this view.
8. It proved to be a tight fit, but the lighting circuit will go in. Virtually no heat is generated so the close proximity to the sides of the model is of no concern. Secured with a sticky pad to the sides of the cabin, the unit can be connected to the flashing LED dressed up as a tail light.

9. Basic wiper pick ups are all that this model requires for constant operation of the tail light. Layouts operated with a DCC system have constant track power at 16v AC, at about 2.5 to 5 Amps. The flashing taillight uses a fraction of that current supply and relies on the circuit to rectify it and reduce the voltage.

planked floors. The cabin walls and doors are shortened as a result and need to be corrected if modelling the verandah areas. Once the model is stripped into constituent parts, each can be worked on and painted separately.

Painting and finishing the 'Queen Mary' brake van

In addition to the base EWS maroon colour, there are a surprising number of small details to paint in different colours. However, given that the required number of coats of maroon to achieve acceptable coverage will clog the detail that we have either gone to a lot of trouble to add or save, it is worth giving each individual sub-assembly a quick spray with Halfords' oxide coloured plastic primer.

EWS gold is applied in a narrow band above the duckets and to the ends of the verandah roof. Note, by observation of the prototype photographs, how the painters at Toton applied EWS gold to the uprights that support the verandah roof, simply to make our lives a little more challenging! The wooden batten along the edge of the roof has an orange warning stripe applied, this is not continuous as some

Open veranda doors and weathering adds some character to an out of the box model. It seems strange that this was not explored by Bachmann to give the model more character but instead, it designed a huge ballast weight to fill not only the cabin but verandas as well, limiting the potential of this part of the model unless it is modified.

of the batten was missing from the full-size wagon.

Transfers are from a mix of different types found on numerous sheets supplied by Model Master Professional and Fox Transfers including HEA transfer sheets and Fox transfers sheets number 4979/1 and 4979/2, which shows the lack of modern transfers for simple number, TOPS and data panel

sets for many EWS prototypes in 2008.

The elements have taken their toll on this wagon, with corrosion appearing at the base of the plating on the wagons ends and the underframe. This was represented by dry brushing Railmatch dark rust onto the desired area. General grime was used to show the planking, which was applied using a washing technique and paints of differing grey hues, mostly dark with a touch of brake dust. Humbrol matt varnish was used to seal the paint and transfers in, to prevent them from being rubbed off by handling when the wagon is in service.

Bachmann POA and SSA

Both POA and SSA codes have been used on the same generic wagon in the past and the SSA code is now used on the rebuilt 51t former 'Standard Railfreight' two-axle box scrap wagons in the 470xxx number sequence as operated by EWS today. The SSA code was applied to the wagons when they were taken into BR ownership.

Bachmann offers one of the two main versions of this wagon, the BSC friction pedestal suspension variant which captures the chunky appearance of the

When Bachmann first released the POA (RLS5000-5099), the wagon was modelled in 'as converted' or built condition. This version of the model is an early variant with the correct markings, paint colour and no angled plates fitted to the horizontal ribs.

The level of detail is very good, especially around the underframe.

wagon was modelled in 'as converted' or built condition. The deflector plates added retrospectively to prevent build-up of scrap on the ribs was also tooled into later models of the POA and the version coded SSA. Earlier models (and the Cambrian kit) can be modified by adding pieces of 10thou strip along the top edges of the horizontal ribs.

Overall, the Bachmann model is well modelled and accurate. Indeed, earlier in the book, the use of the underframe on PNA bodies as a cross-conversion was demonstrated.

The later EWS rebuilds are yet to be represented in model form. However, it's a simple conversion of the Bachmann wagon, by simply modifying the corner plates and the rib arrangement on the end panels. The horizontal ribs themselves are strengthened with the same 10thou styrene strip mentioned earlier. Painting in EWS colours and weathering completes the job.

former POA wagons. The model represents only the first 100, which were constructed from redundant BSC PGA wagons with disc brakes and stepped solebars. Their original running numbers were RLS 5000-99. To model the remaining 60 POA and SSA wagons built with Gloucester suspension and numbered RLS 5921-5980, the Cambrian kit is a good place to start.

When Bachmann first released the POA, as seen in the photographs, the

This is an EWS SSA conversion based on the Bachmann model, where simple pieces of styrene strip have been used to modify the body to represent the strengthening of the ribs, especially at the point were body and underframe meet. Note the strengthened corner plates.

LEFT: Search through the Hornby catalogue and older models treated to quality paint jobs can be found. In 2008, Hornby reissued its ferry van model as a ZSX departmental vehicle. Like the PGA wagon, it can be detailed and enhanced with cast and etched details.

BELOW: Brake vans are popular subjects and Hornby has several in its range. They tend to be older toolings and require work to remove moulding lines and to add additional details to enhance their appearance. This is a nicely finished version of the former Airfix/Dapol LMS brake van decorated as a BR departmental vehicle.

More brake van departmental vehicles modelled using Hornby's BR brake van model. Both liveries are authentic and some work could be made to adjust certain details such as buffers and axleboxes to match these ZTRs.

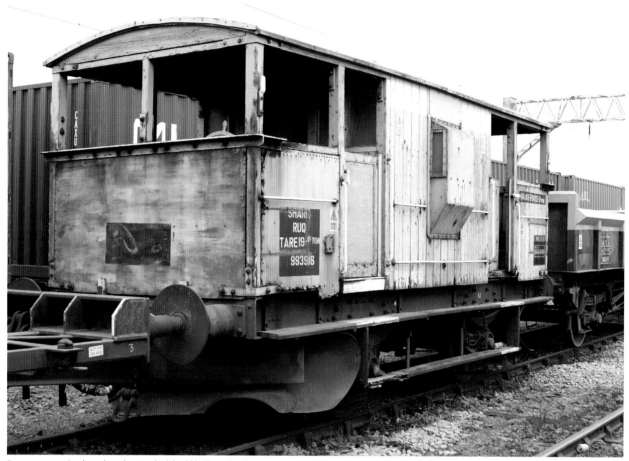

Fancy a conversion based on the Hornby 'Shark' ballast plough brake van? RUQ No. 993916 is a Diagram 1/597 van constructed by the Birmingham RC&W Co in 1957. The plywood ends and sides are repairs replacing the original planks. Note the self-contained buffers and roller bearing axleboxes. It has lost its upright vacuum pipes and has air brake pipes, hence the code RUQ: no brakes (except handbrake) but through air pipe.

Brake and axlebox detail. Those roller bearing axle boxes are not original to Diagram 1/597.

Note the rusting effect on the ploughs and the fact that this van is no longer expected to contribute brake force.

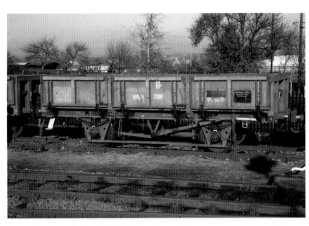

ZBA No. DB 972013 is a typical example of a 'Rudd'.

RIGHT: An interesting feature of this type of wagon is that the livery faded to pale grey and yellow pretty quickly. Add a layer of rusty grime to the mix and DB 977091 is what you get.

Brake and axleguard detail of a typical 'Rudd'.

RIGHT: An unidentified BYA is photographed on the main line. Unremarkable except for the new hood and the overall grimy weathering on the rest of the wagon.

BRA No. 964022 was photographed at Bescot in near original condition.

Not all BDAs find use on steel traffic. BDA No. 950222 was photographed loaded with aluminium at Fort William yard.

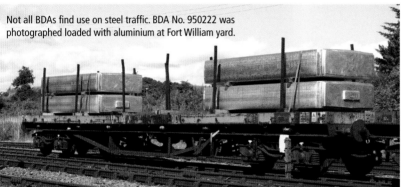

ABOVE LEFT: The lightweight hoods on BYA and BRA wagons are easily damaged. Some have been replaced with unpainted new ones as seen in this April 2008 shot of unidentified wagons. That would make an interesting variation on the Bachmann model. The rest of the wagon is in the usual grimy condition.

ABOVE: Bachmann has released models of the air-braked bogie bolster wagon (BDA family) which is an air braked rebuild of the former 'Bogie Bolster D' wagons fitted with Y25 bogies. They remain in traffic as of 2008 on various flows. BEA No. 950540 is a good example of the type. The BDA wagon saw modifications with different bolster positions which could be represented on the Bachmann wagon. Also, note the brake lever on this particular wagon.

BELOW: Dapol was working on a model of the telescopic hood wagon at the time of writing. It will feature two sliding hoods and coil loads. It should be in the shops by the time you read this.

LEFT: A wagon popular with modellers is the BAA, a steel carrying type which sees use on various flows carrying coils in cradles, slab, blooms and bars. They are equipped with a heavier duty version of the FTB6 bogie. It would make an ideal companion to the Bachmann Class 37/5, and ViTrains Class 37/7 models together with Hornby Class 56 and 60s. How long will it be before we see an off-the-shelf model of a BAA?

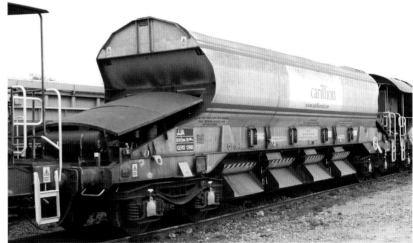

RIGHT: The large JJA auto-ballaster wagons have been proposed by Bachmann in its 2008-9 release programme. They have been adorned in several different liveries, such as GERS 12905 seen in this photograph.

BELOW: Modellers are still waiting for a ready to run BBA and variations on this theme too! This is BBA No.910395. At present time, kits for both the BAA and BBA are available from Cambrian Models.

No such thing as a mixed freight? EWS Class 66 No.66 109 wheels a mixed train of ferry vans, BEAs and BDAs through Barnetby in July 2007. A single TTA is seen in the train behind the locomotive.

JJAs are single wagons equipped with draw gear at both ends and fitted with Y25 bogies. There are variations, depending on the type of hopper – either cut-down or with a generator compartment for powering a train of them. This is GERS 12937 in Railtrack colours.

A CDA dressed in ECC blue livery showing the typical weathering and clay spillage effects that these wagons commonly suffer in their day-to-day duties. The slots seen on this side of the wagon are not represented on the Hornby model.

CDA 375014 was photographed at St. Blazey depot in typically weathered condition. Note the patch where the ECC logo had been removed.

A typical 1990s ballast train was photographed at Wooton Rivers on the Berks & Hants in May 1997. The train consists of a mix of former aggregate wagons coded 'Barbell' and 'Zander'. The former are old 27 ton stone wagons once used on aggregate traffic and offered by Hornby in yellow grey livery as a re-issue of its 27t mineral wagon model. The latter can only be constructed from scratch or kit-bashed.

RIGHT: YTX No. 56299 has seen better days and appears tatty despite the application of EWS livery undertaken at Toton WRD in April 1998.

BELOW LEFT: One verandah door is plated over, but in general the woodwork is in reasonable condition.

BELOW RIGHT: This is a view of side 'A', the airbrake equipment, cylinder and reservoir tank can be clearly seen. The 8' 0" 'steam' bogies appear to be in original condition. The data panels show that this van is being maintained, the last inspection being in February 2002.

Ballast and spoil wagons can appear particularly battered because mechanical grabs are used to unload them. The bodysides are distorted and most of the original paint finish has flaked away to reveal a dark brown rust with traces of lighter coloured rust in places. The rust is dry and dusty-looking, which means that this could be modelled using the technique involving a mixture of gouache, weathering powder, MicroSol and hairspray, applied with a sponge in subtle layers with colour variation. This MKA was photographed at Newport on April 26, 2004.

This final chapter looks at some important elements to making the best of ready-to-run wagons. The first part looks further at weathering techniques including grime and rusting. This is followed up with those tasks required for 'commissioning' your models ready for traffic, including the use of Kadee couplings to enhance operations, using the NEM coupling pockets, troubleshooting coupling issues and looking at smooth operation of the wagons themselves.

Weathering techniques

Cosmetic sponges and hairspray are some of the materials used by extreme weathering enthusiasts and fall into the category of 'embarrassing purchases' (together with polystyrene ceiling tiles and cork floor tiles) that modellers frequently find themselves having to make. Nothing gets you noticed in Superdrug quicker than making a purchase of cosmetic sponges. As the (usually) young and pretty shop assistant looks at you closely to see how well you

have applied your foundation that morning, little do they know that weathering is the intended use for the sponges, for is it not a form of make-up that we are applying to our models? Not that I know anything about make-up!

It was during a particularly intense session of surfing for new ideas that I came across several interesting web sites, hosted by private individuals, who describe some useful and, in some instances, pretty extreme weathering techniques with astounding results.

When I first surfed into Rich Divizio's 'Model Trains Weathered', I was astounded at the quality of the work and the level of realism that been achieved with otherwise quite ordinary freight car models. The site included useful advice on a variety of weathering effects including rust pitting, straining, rust runs, general grime and spillage. Graffiti gets a look in too, including techniques for dulling down and weathering 'tagged' freight cars.

I decided to have a go at some of the techniques after 'data mining' individual threads and making notes on how different modellers achieved different techniques that would be of value to my modelling. It goes to show that research goes beyond number sequences and counting the bolt heads. The key areas that modellers appear to be concentrating on are 'fantasy' projects, where models are weathered according to taste and preference but without actually following a particular prototype vehicle. As you may have guessed, the other method is to examine pictures of prototype rail vehicles and copy them as closely as possible, including graffiti, patching, fading and rusting. One thing is clear, there is no desire to create a collection of rust

Rust pitting and streaks on the end of an OBA wagon. Note how dark the rust pitted areas are and the translucent effect of the staining – some of the original colour still shows through.

buckets and the application of these techniques is both subtle and realistic, although some of the techniques may be too heavy for the majority of British outline freight wagons.

I was particularly interested in the rusting techniques for models representing prototypes that would be exposed to physical damage, such as spoil wagons or where brake dust has resulted in an overall dusting of rust stains over a wagon or container. A second area of interest is the use of general weathering techniques to tone down or 'dull down' containers and wagons with relatively bright liveries and to represent the grime that collects in corners of ribs and other raised details.

Useful materials used by weathering enthusiasts

- Cosmetic sponges have a close cellular structure, which makes them particularly good for achieving certain textures with paint and mixtures of paint and weathering powder. They are easy to clean after use and may be reused many times. They are usually wedge shaped with a narrow edge useful for subtle weathering.
- Hairspray is used as an adhesive and as a sealant by some modellers. The

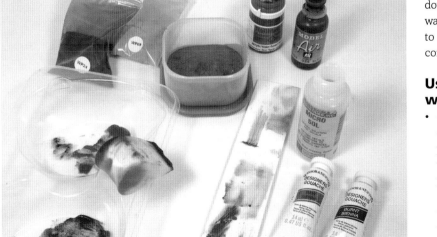

A selection of materials used for weathering and rusting effects including cosmetic sponges, weathering powders and artists' paint.

type sold in pump action bottles is regarded as the best because some techniques require the blending of hairspray and paint which would be very difficult to do with hairspray from an aerosol.

- Acrylic varnish is commonly used as a sealant to protect finished weathering, although modellers should be aware that it can reduce the effectiveness of weathering powders and is known to completely eliminate the effects of pastel chalk. It does, however, prevent the loss of weathering through repeated handling of the models.

- Proper weathering powders which are adhesive have an important role to play and in the UK, Finishing Touches offers a range of powders under its Eazi-Products label.

- Acrylic paints have certain applications and good weathering colours are available from Finishing Touches, Railmatch and Vallejo.

- Artist's materials used with these techniques include designer gouache (water based oil paint), oil paints (preferably fast drying such as Windsor & Newton Griffin Alkyd) and the appropriate thinner. Colours most commonly used are Burnt Sienna and Raw Sienna which find use in rusting techniques. Such paints are slightly translucent when applied in thin coats and the colour built up through successive application, ideal for rust streaking and staining.

- Microscale Microsol is commonly used as a thinning and flow agent with weathering powders, acrylic, oil and gouache paint.

Not wishing to turn all of my personal collection into rust buckets, I generally limit rusting work to minor pitting, gouging, streaking and staining. The tools shown here are all that I use together with the make up sponge.

After all painting and transfer work is complete, the wagons are prepared for a wash of dark grey and dark rust to create general grime. Sometimes, grime can be the result of sun bleaching, so choose colours with care.

Weathering techniques

- **Toning down**

  Bright liveries, such as those found on containers can be made to appear more realistic by simply toning them down. This is achieved by the use of washes of thinned dark grey (avoid black!) paint which is then wiped away to leave traces of paint in corners and around fittings such as hinges.

- **General grime**

  Many modellers apply adhesive weathering powders directly to a model and then assume that that is the end of the process. Many modellers in the United States take a different view. Weathering powders can be streaked and moved around with the use of water, isopropyl alcohol (assuming that it will not attack and damage any underlying layers of acrylic paint) and MicroSol. This works the weathering powders into corners and other raised details creating grimy effects. Wipe off the excess with a rag to leave grime in

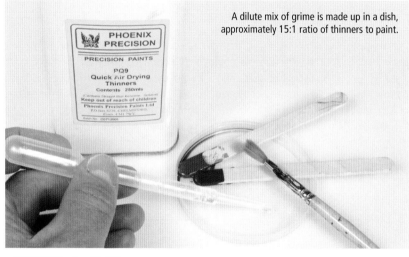

A dilute mix of grime is made up in a dish, approximately 15:1 ratio of thinners to paint.

Some wagons are washed with grime colours and streaked in a downwards motion before being left to dry.

RIGHT: Others are flooded with the grime mixture!

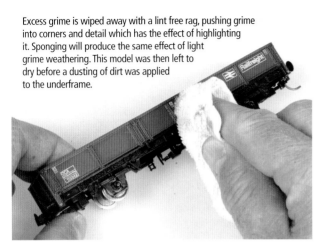

Excess grime is wiped away with a lint free rag, pushing grime into corners and detail which has the effect of highlighting it. Sponging will produce the same effect of light grime weathering. This model was then left to dry before a dusting of dirt was applied to the underframe.

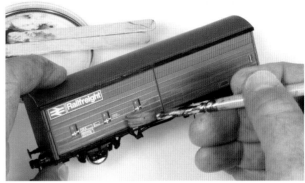

A pale wash is applied to create a bleaching effect on a factory applied finish. The same can be achieved with airbrushing, or using pale colours when first painting the wagon.

the corners. This will take the shine off bright coloured liveries and help make the model more realistic. Both the toning down and griming of a model is regarded as the first steps in the weathering process and should be applied to a matt finished surface.

- **General rusting**

There are instances when a freight vehicle or container is subject to conditions where a general layer of rust coats one or more surfaces. Frequently, the tops of containers have a thin layer of rusty grime resulting from prolonged exposure to the maritime environment. Brake dust also rusts and wagons that are not cleaned will appear to have a layer of relatively dark, grimy rust all over an otherwise intact paint finish. It's not always uniform in colour or in application, but sometimes streaked and sometimes quite even in appearance. This is where your cosmetic sponges come into play once again.

A technique I have tried is to apply thinned enamel paint using a dabbing action with a cosmetic sponge or washed on with a broad flat paintbrush. Either use dark grey on its own or a mix of dark rust and grey. The paint is thinned to about 15:1 thinners to paint for a true wash. Oil paint can also be used in the same way to achieve a heavier application of rust.

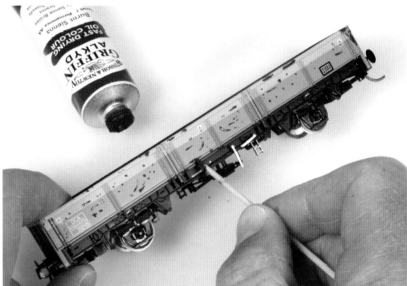

Rust pitting and streaking is an important weathering effect and there are many different ways of achieving this. One method involves the use of fast drying oil based artists' paint which is spotted onto the model with a cocktail stick.

- **Rust pitting and paint damage**

This is a real favourite of mine and there are many different techniques used to achieve pitting and rusting from paint damage, including some that take many hours to achieve. My favourite is to apply spots and thin lines of Burnt Sienna oil paint to the sides of a wagon that has already been toned down with very thin washes of grey and dark rust, using a cocktail stick or micro brush. Before the paint has dried, I brush the sides of the wagon in a downward direction with a flat brush lightly loaded with thinners. The result is a lighter rust stain originating from an area of darker rust pitting as a result of rain water action. The oil paint is left to dry for several days and the model sealed with matt varnish to protect the weathering work.

Rusting resulting from the blistering of old paint is usually a very dark colour and will vary in shade. Like all of these things, there are many different ways of achieving this effect. One method is to use a mixture of hairspray, gouache, weathering powders and MicroSol mixed together

This PNA was to be subjected to light rust pitting. Burnt Sienna fast drying oil paint is applied with a cocktail stick in spots and lines on the previously grimed wagon body. Although the grime is subtle, place the model beside a pristine one and you will soon notice the difference!

Rust staining resulting from the action of rainwater on rust pits can be modelled by streaking the artists' oil paint by dragging the oil paint down with a flat brush very lightly loaded with thinner. This PNA is being treated with Burnt Sienna which streaks nicely into different iron oxide (rust!) shades.

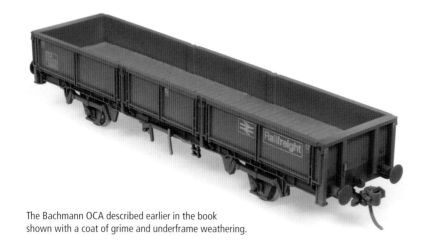

The Bachmann OCA described earlier in the book shown with a coat of grime and underframe weathering.

Apart from a coat of grime, painting of the interior and rusting effects, the body of this Bachmann ZKA is unmodified, demonstrating how weathering can add character to ready to run models.

until it is gritty. This is applied with a cosmetic sponge in a dabbing motion to create the effect of old, dry, dusty rust which has resulted from the loss of paint from a metal surface. It can be applied as thin or as heavy as is desired and can be streaked or left as it is. Sometimes it is useful to have several different mixes available which are subtly different in colour to build up the layers. This technique has a particular application on ballast, spoil and mineral wagons, something I resisted doing to those test sample models of the Hornby 'Rudd', 'Tope' and 'Clam!'

The 'process'

The basic 'layering' process that I have adopted is based on my gathering of knowledge from Model Trains Weathered and other websites, together with much experimentation of my own. It has progressed beyond the two-stage weathering described earlier in the book with the 'Dogfish' ballast wagon. A record card is written up with details of the process, so it can be referred to during the weathering, so a consistent finish can be achieved over time. I will still use dry-brushing and airbrush weathering techniques to complement the following technique.

1. Once the model is painted in the

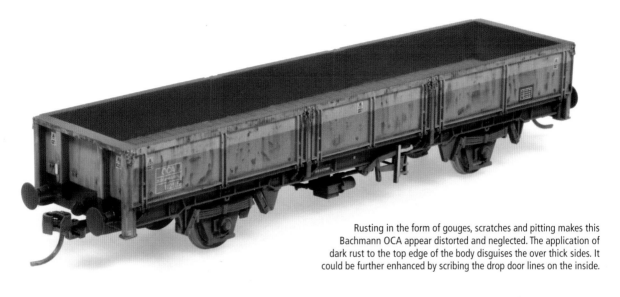

Rusting in the form of gouges, scratches and pitting makes this Bachmann OCA appear distorted and neglected. The application of dark rust to the top edge of the body disguises the over thick sides. It could be further enhanced by scribing the drop door lines on the inside.

Rust on a different Bachmann ZKA wagon.

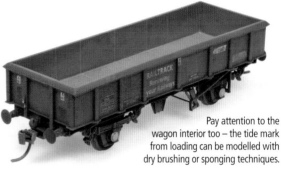

Pay attention to the wagon interior too – the tide mark from loading can be modelled with dry brushing or sponging techniques.

intended livery, finished with transfers, had the interior painted where appropriate and varnished, graffiti could be added to the model together with patch painting to represent repairs.

2. Application of grime consisting of 15:1 thinned paint is applied next, to tone the model down and remove the 'brightness' from modern liveries, particularly on freight wagons. This process can be very subtle indeed and could be followed by the application of paint patches representing repairs and more recent graffiti 'tagging' if desired. Thin washes such as this can be applied in layers to build up the grime if so desired, but it takes time, as it is best to wait for each wash to dry, so the result can be carefully considered before moving on with the next step.

3. General rusting can be applied on some surfaces, particularly where brake dust has rusted over time or there is exposed metal in areas such as hopper interiors. This should blend with the general application of grime and could be further patch painted and graffitied.

4. Rust pitting and streaking on those wagons subject to physical damage.

5. Weathering from the loading and discharging of wagons. This includes spillage of powders, liquids and dusting from aggregates and ballast.

6. The underframes and bogies of wagons can be weathered using similar techniques.

7. I will sometimes apply a dusting of brake dust to complete the job, together with a thin coat of varnish to seal it all in and protect the wagon during handling.

Extreme weathering websites

Model Trains Weathered:
www.modeltrainsweathered.com
Mellow Mike's weathering site:
www.mellowmike.com

Using Kadee couplings
No.5 Kadees

General dissatisfaction with tension lock couplings fitted as standard to British outline OO scale models has led to the increased popularity of Kadee couplers. Kadees are modelled on a US prototype and were originally designed to suit US-outline models. However, their neat appearance, together with durability and operational flexibility has seen their adoption by modellers throughout the

Fitting a Kadee No.5 to the Hornby PGA hopper wagon

1. Commence by popping the centre spring into the coupler box. Be sure to fit it the correct way up. Assembly of each individual coupler should take no longer than a couple of minutes.

2. Secure the lid with a tiny quantity of liquid solvent cement applied with a paintbrush. Go gently here – too much solvent will clog the coupling with melted plastic.

3. 'Greas-em', a dry lubricant, is puffed into the coupler box to ensure smooth operation.
4. Once the couplings are assembled and operating smoothly, take the coupling height

gauge and do a first check on the subject wagon. It is possible to attach the gauge to a dedicated length of track if so desired.

world. Kadees are certainly not new, they have been manufactured since 1947 and the range has grown dramatically as Kadee has added different types Including a new 'scale series' and to suit modellers in countries outside the United States. Despite their popularity in the UK, I often receive queries about the use of Kadees and how to fit them to British outline rolling stock, particularly those items not equipped with NEM-362 coupling pockets. Many new models are now released with these coupling pockets, which makes the use of special Kadees, the No.17 to 21 series, relatively straightforward.

The No.5 Kadee is designed for the freelance conversion of almost any model, providing there is sufficient room for the coupler box and it is a good place for newcomers to Kadees to make a start. The coupler box contains the centring spring and a method of fixing the coupler to the frame or chassis of the model. One

5. Remove the tension lock coupling and see if the headstocks are high enough to take the coupler without modification. The flat end of the gauge is used for this purpose. It gives an idea if the headstocks have to be notched to

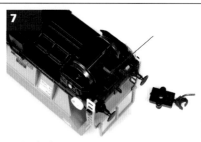

accommodate the coupling box or if the mounting pad of styrene should protrude below the headstocks by a few thou.
6. Once an idea of coupling mounting has been determined with the gauge, snip away all the

tension lock mounting.
7. Build up a pad on which the coupling will be fitted, using 20thou black styrene glued to the underside of the wagon. Use the height gauge to achieve the right amount of padding.

8. This shows the No.5 fitted. The back face of the coupler should be level with the buffer faces for reliable operation, both propelling and hauling, on 3' curves. Pull the coupler out for sharper curvature. Note how the box of the No.5 coupler extends beyond the headstocks,

which some modellers find undesirable.
9. An alternative to the good old No.5 is one of the 40 series couplers with the same type of coupler box but a wider variety of knuckles. This shows a long shank knuckle. The series includes offset couplers, short, medium and long

shanks too!
10. Test the installation with the height gauge. That tool is your best friend when doing this sort of task. The red line shows the fitting with the back face of the coupler level with the buffer faces.

of the problems with freelance conversions is that almost every model requires a different approach, unless it's a generic family of models. To describe the conversion technique for every available off-the-shelf wagon would require a book of many pages.

The key principles of freelance coupling conversions are described in detail below and the technique is basically the same for each and every model. Some experimentation is inevitable, but before attempting to convert a model for the first time, you must be aware of a couple of principles. It is important that you forget about mounting couplings to the bogies of bogie wagons, as Kadees simply do not work that way unless a NEM coupling pocket is provided on the bogie and even then this is not ideal. Freelance coupling conversions should all be applied to the frame of the model so that coupling forces are transmitted through the

wagon frame, leaving the bogies to work independently over the track.

Kadees are designed to be fitted at a specific height from the rail, which enables the use of delayed uncoupling devices *via* dropper pins fitted to the knuckle. Naturally, it is desirable to mount all of your couplings at the same height to ensure effective operation. Kadee supply a special gauge which can be set on the track of your choice and rolling stock checked against this, to see what work needs to be done and then to verify the installation once work is complete. The value of a Kadee No.205 coupler height gauge cannot be over-emphasised. It is through the fitting of Kadee couplers and the use of the coupler height gauge that modellers discovered that some NEM-362 pockets are out of specification on some RTR models. The coupler height gauge will ensure that your installation is correct and will match the other vehicles on

When buying couplings, grab a few packs of spares too! Always useful to have to hand, just in case.

your layout.

Freelance conversions involve the fitting of the coupler box to a pad of styrene. The number of pieces depends on the model and available space. To save time, purchase a pack of Evergreen 40thou x 250 thou strip (pack No.149) from which you can cut mounting pad material. Some 20 thou material will also be useful for fine adjustment. Black would be the preferred colour for

Fitting a Kadee No.5 to the Bachmann POA/SSA scrap carrier

1. The Bachmann four-axle scrap carrier is a popular model and quite an accurate one too. It is not equipped with NEM coupler pockets making it an ideal candidate for conversion with a No.5 or a No. 46 Kadee coupler. No modifications to the

headstocks are required.
2. Pare away the moulded coupling mount with a sharp scalpel until it is level with the bottom edge of the headstocks, keeping your fingers behind the blade. To avoid damaging detail you

wish to keep, use a sharp blade and pare material away in small amounts.
3. Use a smooth-cut file to finish work on the coupling mount. The mount can be used instead of a pad of styrene to fix the new coupler.

4. Drill a 2mm diameter hole through the centre of the moulded coupling mount.
5. The new Kadee is fitted to the pared down

coupling mount using a plastic 8BA screw which is a type supplied by Kadee. This has the advantage over brass screws in being easy to

trim.
6. The finished job! It takes about 20 minutes to complete this coupling conversion.

styrene – for obvious reasons. Fit the couplings before weathering the model so their appearance can be 'blended in' with the rest of the model.

The photographs on pages 170, 171 and 172 demonstrate the use of 'The Ol' Reliable', No.5 Kadee, which remains a firm favourite for the freelance conversion of British outline models. The techniques can then be applied to other wagons.

NEM-362 standard Kadee couplings - The No. 17-20 series

Increasingly, we are seeing the application of NEM standards to OO scale British-outline models, NEM-362 coupling boxes are just one example of the beneficial adoption of European standards to new British models, although many older models are yet to be retrospectively fitted. There are many benefits in the adoption of a standard that allows for the interchange of different coupling heads, which is the principle behind NEM-362. Kadee has developed four types of coupling with swallowtail shanks that are designed to fit the coupling box specified in NEM-362. Kadees must be fitted at a specific height to ensure that they function correctly, much in the same manner that couplings on the real railways need to, so that they can function with each other. Unfortunately, the application of NEM-362 on UK-outline models has been subject to some strange interpretation, resulting in many new ready-to-run wagons being fitted with NEM-362 pockets that are either too high or too low. Because the tension lock coupling remains the standard in the UK, the manufacturers adjust the coupling head to suit the situation rather than correct non-compliant coupling pockets.

If a model with a non-standard coupling box is used on a layout with other models equipped with tension lock couplings, the modeller should experience no problems other than those inherent with tension lock couplings. Attempt to replace the tension lock coupling with a Kadee coupler and any mismatch with the coupling box becomes apparent. This can be very frustrating and defeats the objective of adopting published standards.

NEM-362 standard

NEM (Normes Européennes de Modélisme) European Standards for Modelling have been developed and compiled by MOROP, The European Union of Model Railroad and Railroad Fans. MOROP was founded in Genoa in

---

Fitting a Kadee No. 5 to the Hornby PCA

1. To determine if any modifications to the headstocks are necessary to accommodate Kadee couplers, the model is checked against the Kadee No.205 height gauge. As can be seen, the headstocks appear to clear the knuckle on

the height gauge.
2. A sharp scalpel makes short work of the moulded coupling box. This makes room for mounting pads made from pieces of 40thou styrene. In the case of the PCA, three pieces of

styrene are required.
3. The mounting pad is located directly inboard of the headstocks and they should be level with the bottom edge of the headstocks.

4. The coupler is glued into place with a small quantity of liquid solvent cement. Alternatively, the coupler can be mounted with an 8BA screw.
5. It is not necessary to retain the fixing loops moulded to the side of the coupler boxes. In this

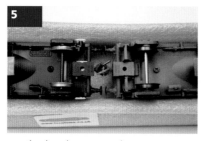

case they have been removed.
6. Two Hornby PCAs: the one nearest the camera is a rebuilt model fitted with modified brake detail. Kadees were fitted to this model as work progressed and are weathered as part of the

general finishing of the model. Kadee couplers will take sparing amounts of paint - such as weathering colours to match the rest of the model. Excessive paint will inevitably cause problems with the coupling and uncoupling action, so be careful!

Bachmann EWS HTA coal hoppers

1. The Bachmann HTA wagon is an excellent model with NEM-362 compatible coupling boxes supplied. The factory-fitted EZMate coupling is not at the correct height for use with Kadee couplers.

2. The seemingly arbitrary height of the EZMate couplings supplied with the model caused problems for some modellers. The centreline of the coupling is

12mm from the rail; approximately 3mm greater than the operational height of Kadee couplings. Examination of works drawings shows a height of 964mm to the knuckle coupling fitted to the prototype, which equates to 12.5mm to the nearest half millimetre in 4mm scale. So the model is scale in this respect, if operationally irritating from a modeller's point of view.

3. The bogies are fitted with NEM coupling adapter pocket sockets and so conversion to either tension lock couplings or Kadee No.18 and 19 types is possible without difficulty.

4. The simplest way to remove the EZMate couplings supplied with the model is to remove the bogies first to obtain access to the keeper plate and screw.

5. When the NEM coupling pocket adapter is fitted, Kadee couplers are a simple plug-in fitting. A small piece of 10 thou styrene fitted between the swallowtail shank and the bottom of the coupler box will ensure it does not 'droop' out of gauge.

6. Prototype HTA wagons are not equipped with buffers. With no buffers in place on either the model or the prototype, the risk of buffer locking is

non-existent making it possible to fit the shortest of the NEM-362 compatible Kadee couplers. The wagons shown in this picture are fitted with No.17 Kadee couplers. Wagons run within a rake could have the dropper bars removed from the couplers to prevent wagons parting from the train should the train come to a stand with the wagons over an uncoupling magnet.

Hornby 'merry-go-round' wagons

1. The Hornby HAA model and those derived from the basic underframe are equipped with NEM-362 coupling boxes at the correct height. The boxes are set back from the headstocks very slightly which, together with the length of buffer, means that a long shank Kadee would be the best choice.

2. A No.20 Kadee is probably the most practical choice for this model. This demonstrates how easy the use of coupler boxes can be. Simply plug the swallowtail end of the coupling into the box and you're done!

3. Test the installation against a coupling height gauge. Some coupling boxes fitted to this type of model may have some slack in them resulting in coupling 'droop'.

4. The choice of coupling can be important depending on how sharp the curves are on your layout. If you have very sharp curves you should consider the use of the longest shank as seen in this picture of two Hornby MGR models which have been fitted with No.20 Kadees.

5. No.19 Kadees result in a much closer coupling effect. These models are fitted with sprung buffers so it is theoretically possible to use Kadees with shorter shanks for closer coupling on layouts with sharp curves. It may be necessary to undertake some tests on reverse curves and cross-over junctions before committing to close coupling.

6. Coupling 'droop' is caused by slack in the coupling box. It is possible to tighten things up and ensure that the Kadee coupler rides at the correct height from the running rail. Simply insert a small piece of 10thou styrene between the bottom of the box and the swallowtail shank.

1954 and has since been working on European standards for model railways. Close ties were established between MOROP and the American National Model Railroad Association in 1994 and this clearly was beneficial as far as Kadee was concerned. The NEM-362 standard ('Boîtier pour tête d'attelage interchangeable'), clearly sets out the case for interchangeable coupling heads and the related coupling box, together with the comment that the standard is mandatory for satisfactory operation. For example, the height, length and width of the coupling box is clearly specified, together with the height of the box from the running rail. NEM-362 states that, in HO, the top of the inside of the coupler box should be no greater than 8.5mm from the rail with a tolerance no greater than 0.2mm. As we have seen throughout this book, there are some UK-outline models fitted with coupling boxes that do not conform to this standard. When checking the fit of coupling pockets, do so on a model fitted with its original wheels. Models converted with closer-to-scale wheels may find that differences in wheel diameter may make a difference and such differences should be taken into account.

Kadee 17-20 series couplings

Kadee recognised the need to produce some couplings with NEM-362 compliant swallow tail shanks, thus opening a potential new market in Europe for its products. The adoption of NEM-362 by British-outline manufacturers means that, in theory, there is a much simpler method of using Kadee couplers on British outline stock than the freelance fitting of Kadee No.5 couplers described above. In the main this is the case and it has become a simple task to remove the unwanted tension lock coupling from the coupling box and replace it with one of the four Kadee couplers from the No. 17-21 series, or any other swallowtail coupling head for that matter. The coupler head is fitted to the swallowtail shank so its centreline is at the normal Kadee standard height of 9.9mm from the running rail. This means that the dropper bar is 0.8mm from the running rail ensuring that it does not foul switch blades on coupling ramps. The coupler swallowtail shank is intended to be mounted 8.5mm from the rail, exactly the same as the specified dimension of a NEM-362 coupler box. There is very little

Adjusting the Bachmann TTA

1. A good example of the liberal interpretation of the NEM-362 specification can be seen in the 2005 release of the Bachmann TTA tank wagon which has been perpetuated in other models that utilise the same underframe tooling. The coupling pocket is mounted too high from rail level to make the use of compatible Kadee couplers of any value. The standard states that, in HO, the top of the inside of the coupler box should the no greater than 8.5 mm with a tolerance no greater than 0.2 mm.

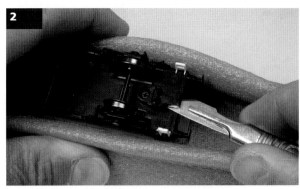

2. It is possible to remove the coupling box from the model by carefully inserting a scalpel blade between the underframe floor and adapter box. With careful twisting of the blade, the box should pop off. Carefully examine the moulded bracket from which you have removed the coupling box. The screw visible in the bracket is actually used to secure the wagon body to the underframe and not the moulded bracket itself. This makes removal of the bracket - so that it can be fitted at the correct height - almost impossible without having to modify the body securing method too.

3. However, not all is lost because there is sufficient room under the headstocks to fit a variety of different Kadee couplers. This is based on the assumption that the NEM coupling pocket mount is of no use on this model. A No.205 height gauge is used to determine how a replacement

coupling would fit.
4. After trimming a small spigot of plastic back down to floor level, a piece of 40thou styrene is glued to the floor. This will form the mounting pad for a new Kadee coupler.

5. The replacement Kadee coupler is glued into place and left to harden for a couple of hours. If you wish to test the viability before committing to glue, use a small piece of 'Blu-Tak' as a temporary adhesive to check the installation against the height gauge.

6. Unfortunately all of the models based on this underframe will have the same problem. The new MTA open box wagon will need to be worked on in a similar manner.

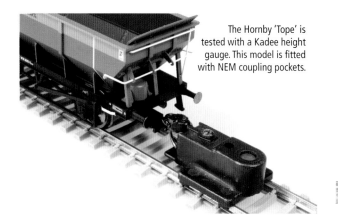

The Hornby 'Tope' is tested with a Kadee height gauge. This model is fitted with NEM coupling pockets.

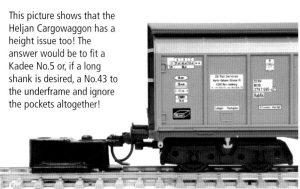

This picture shows that the Heljan Cargowaggon has a height issue too! The answer would be to fit a Kadee No.5 or, if a long shank is desired, a No.43 to the underframe and ignore the pockets altogether!

Bachmann OBA and OCA, together with the Railfreight van models have correctly fitted pockets, but they are fitted to the articulated axleguards, which means they do not align correctly with adjacent wagons depending on curvature of the track. The cure is to fit couplings to the wagon frame.

The Hornby 'Shark' is spot on. Together with the specially adapted plough assembly, there has been a lot of thought put into this area of the model.

Some models such as the Hornby 'Rudd', 'Tope' and 'Clam' have their NEM-362 coupling pockets fitted to a cam mechanism for close coupling. As the wagon passes around a curve, the action of the cam opens the gap between coupled wagons to prevent buffer lock. The Heljan 'Dogfish' ballast hopper is similarly equipped.

Bachmann OBA and OCA wagons can be modified with the NEM coupling pocket fitted to the wagon floor and not the axleguards. This shows the finished result equipped with No.18 Kadees.

margin for error.

The four different couplers differ from each other by having shanks of differing lengths: the No.17 has a short shank for close coupling of stock whilst the No.20 has a long shank for those situations where it is necessary to use the model on sharp curves. There should be a Kadee to suit your particular application. It is useful to have a selection of different Kadees on your work bench to check which is the most suitable for your model. If the curves on your model railway are sharper than 3' radius then it is worth considering the use of the No.20 Kadee on all of your stock to avoid buffer locking. Experience has shown that to prevent buffer locking on layouts with a ruling curve radius of 3', the back face of the knuckle must be in line with the front of the front face of the buffers or the gangway rubbing plate on coaching stock, whichever protrudes the most. Experiment with the four different types of Kadee to find one that meets this criteria, because most British outline models fitted with NEM-362 coupling boxes are different from each other.

Bachmann ZKA (and TTA) underframes fitted with Kadee No.5 couplings instead of the NEM type, because the NEM-362 coupler box is mounted too high on the model. It's easier not to use them at all. As long as they are set to the correct operating height, anything goes!

Non-compliant models

Even when a model is fitted with an NEM-362 coupling box, there is no

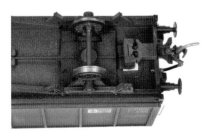

A Bachmann VGA/VKA wagon with the coupling mount separated from the axleguards and glued directly to the wagon underframe. This makes the operation of NEM Kadees more reliable with this genre of Bachmann wagons, because the NEM-362 box is also fitted too high to the VGA.

Should a NEM Kadee appear to droop slightly in the NEM coupling pocket, insert a small fillet of 10thou styrene to tighten things up and lift the coupling head. This usually does the trick for the majority of apparently out-of-specification NEM boxes.

guarantee that it is fitted to the height specified in the standard. In many instances, the non-compliant model has to be modified to bring it into line with the remainder of a collection. In extreme instances the coupling box is removed completely and replaced with a freelance Kadee installation. Models that have non-compliant NEM-362 coupler boxes include the Bachmann VGA/VKA and TTA and other types of wagons derived from the underframe used on that model, including the PNA and MKAs described earlier in the book.

One source of irritation with the NEM-362 boxes supplied on some UK outline models is slack in the coupling box resulting in 'coupling droop'. This is when the Kadee coupler flops in a vertical plane in the pocket and does not sit at the correct operating height. The cure is quite simple: insert a small piece of 10 thou styrene between the swallowtail shank and the bottom of the coupler box to tighten things up.

When wagons derail

The value of back-to-back (Back-to-back) gauges cannot be over emphasised when it comes to reliable performance of rolling stock. Most derailments that occur on exhibition and home-based layouts happen when a wheelset on a particular item of stock is out-of-gauge, or when a piece of track has a defect. Reliability problems with wagons can be avoided by regular and careful maintenance and part of that maintenance regime should include checking every wheelset with a back-to-back gauge on a regular basis as wheelsets can move out of gauge during prolonged use.

As an aside, the same can happen to track which may sustain damage when an exhibition layout is moved or during building and scenery work. This may not be immediately apparent until trains are seen to persistently derail on a particular stretch of track. When that happens, it's a good idea to get the track roller gauges out to see if the rails are distorted or out of alignment.

Given that this book is mostly concerned with ready-to-run wagons, we shall look at the value of back-to-back gauges, which are simple devices for measuring the distance between wheels on a wheelset (a wheelset consists of two wheels mounted to an axle, either with or without a drive gear). In effect, they are an accurately machined block of metal produced to the exact back-to-back measurements for a given gauge. The back of both wheels should sit comfortably against the gauge when they are correctly set and it should be possible to pull the

Derailments can be avoided by using back-to-back gauges. Suspect wheelsets are placed in the gauge and adjusted until the wheels sit snugly against the outside faces. A OO gauge (left) and EM gauge (right) are shown.

A new design of back-to-back gauge for checking back-to-back measurements on rolling stock and locomotive wheelsets is produced by Markits. The design is different to other types of back-to-back gauge in that they are equipped with a convenient handle which makes them easier to use without having to remove wheelsets from rolling stock.

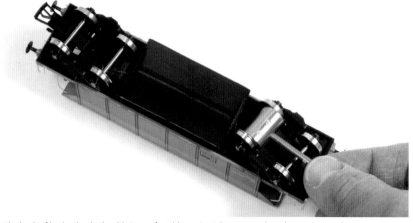

The back of both wheels should sit comfortably against the gauge when they are correctly set, as seen on this Bachmann ballast hopper wagon which has been equipped with Markits 12mm diameter wheels.

gauge clear without effort. If the gauge is loose when inserted between the wheelsets, the wheels are out-of-gauge and should be carefully adjusted along the axle until the rear faces touch the gauge but no more. The same applies if there is insufficient room to insert the gauge between the wheels. One of the dangers of making adjustments to wheelsets is the potential of distorting them, especially if the inner disc of the wheel is composed of plastic and has detail such as spokes.

When adjusting the back-to-back measurement of a given wheelset, ensure that there is an equal amount of axle on either side of each wheel so that the wheels will run in alignment with the others. Apart from regular maintenance, when back-to-back measurements should be checked as a matter of routine, one of the danger signs to look out for during operating sessions is the rogue item of rolling stock or a locomotive that persistently derails on random crossings and turnouts. When a wheelset is incorrectly set, it is likely to refuse to run through flangeways on crossing vees and check rails resulting in a derailment or at least some very jerky and inconsistent running. Derailments at the switch end of the turnout will occur if one back-to-back measurement is too narrow - this will cause a wheel to come into contact

Wheels often 'go out of gauge' because the wheel slips easily on the axle. A simple technique is to remove the wheels from the axle, then 'knurl' the axle between two files before refitting the wheels. The difference is surprising!

with the end of a switch rail. Look out for these signs and be prepared to remove a wagon from the layout for immediate repair or attention after the running session is over. Adjusting a faulty wheelset may be all that it takes to get the errant wagon running smoothly again.

Ballast weight and smooth running

Not all ready-to-run models are equal in terms of weight and there are many discrepancies between different manufacturer's products. Ideally, wagons of about the same size should

weigh the same for the best running. The NMRA devised a simple calculation for weight based on 1 ounce minimum for each wagon and then an additional fixed weight of 0.5 ounce per inch of wagon length in HO scale in its recommended practice RP-20.1, published in 1990. This is technically ideal given that most US-outline freight cars are within a few inches in length of each other excluding specialist cars such as 89' auto-rack cars. Also, they all run on bogies whilst UK-outline modellers have to contend with a variety of different sized wagons, both with bogies and fixed underframes. Many modellers in the United States do not necessarily agree with RP-20.1, but it does work.

The rule of thumb is not to over-ballast your wagons which reduces wear on bearings and locomotives. Add ballast (as 1mm or less diameter lead shot, old car wheel balance weights, self-adhesive weights, etc.) to those that appear to need it and try and keep all wagons of the same length approximately the same weight. Ensure that ballast is evenly distributed so each wagon axle carries an equal load. If the NMRA system appeals to you, visit: www.nmra.org/standards/sandrp/rp-20_1.html for more information.

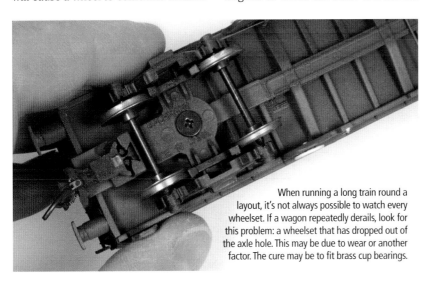

When running a long train round a layout, it's not always possible to watch every wheelset. If a wagon repeatedly derails, look for this problem: a wheelset that has dropped out of the axle hole. This may be due to wear or another factor. The cure may be to fit brass cup bearings.

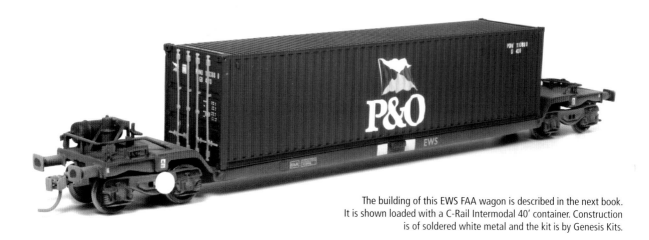

The building of this EWS FAA wagon is described in the next book.
It is shown loaded with a C-Rail Intermodal 40' container. Construction
is of soldered white metal and the kit is by Genesis Kits.

A casual glance through any book on prototype wagons will quickly reveal that there are a huge number of modern wagons from the 1970s onwards not represented by off-the-shelf products. The gaps are huge, one of them being revenue wagons for steel, chemicals, petroleum, international and intermodal traffic. Whilst the mainstream manufacturers are taking more interest in modern wagons, much to their credit, the development of new models is a slow process and many wagons may not be produced in ready-to-run plastic for many years. Guessing as to what may appear next is difficult at best.

Kits are often the best way to obtain those important 'signature' wagons for your fleet which are not available off-the-shelf, at the cost of time and materials to build and finish them. At the extreme end, one can resort to what some modellers jokingly call 'flat-pack' wagons. In other words, scratch-building with styrene sheet and strip together with the use of readily available components for buffers, bogies, brake gear and so on. Then there are things like extreme conversions, cross-kitting, white metal kits, brass kits, multimedia kits and a whole host of detailing components to explore.

The construction of composite plastic and brass
kits will be described. This example is a PFA
container kit by DC Kits.

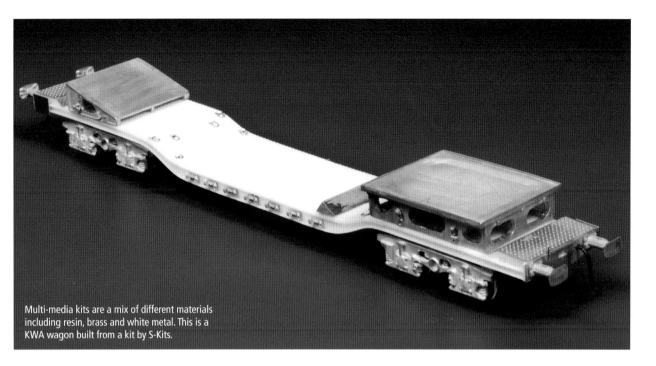

Multi-media kits are a mix of different materials including resin, brass and white metal. This is a KWA wagon built from a kit by S-Kits.

Acknowledgements

No book like this can be compiled and written without the assistance and help of friends, colleagues, professional railwaymen and fellow modellers. I would like to thank the following for their kind assistance.

Manufacturers

Simon Kohler – Hornby Hobbies plc
Dennis Lovett – Bachmann Europe plc
Merl Evans – Bachmann Europe plc
George Ansell – S-Kits

John Flower – A1 Models
Graham Shaw, formerly of Shawplan Models. Enjoy your retirement, Graham!
Ken Bridger – Genesis Kits
Arran Aird – C-Rail Intermodal and fellow wagon enthusiast

Fellow modelling enthusiasts

Tom Smith
Graeme Elgar

In the office

Richard Wilson and Ryan Housden for their support, proofing and design work, not to mention oodles of patience with my endless requests!

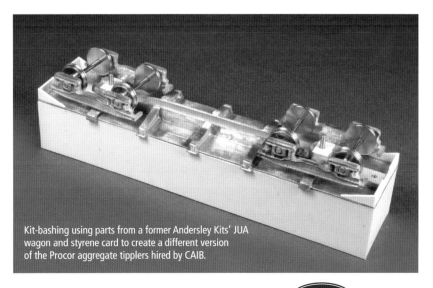

Kit-bashing using parts from a former Andersley Kits' JUA wagon and styrene card to create a different version of the Procor aggregate tipplers hired by CAIB.

THE END

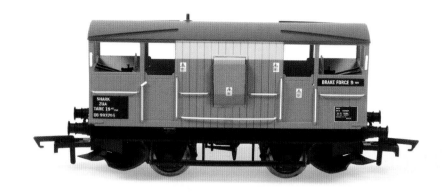

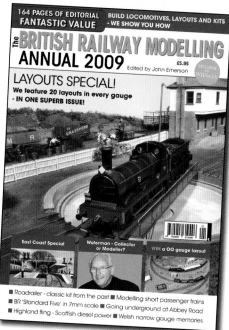
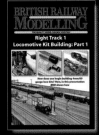

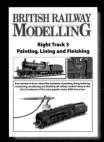